Gilbert Burnet

Three Letters Concerning the Present State of Italy, Written in the Year 1687

Gilbert Burnet

Three Letters Concerning the Present State of Italy, Written in the Year 1687

ISBN/EAN: 9783337721008

Printed in Europe, USA, Canada, Australia, Japan

Cover: Foto ©Suzi / pixelio.de

More available books at **www.hansebooks.com**

THREE
LETTERS

Concerning the

Preſent State

O F

ITALY,

Written in the Year 1687.

I. *Relating* to the Affair of MOLINOS,
and the QUIETISTS.

II. *Relating* to the INQUISITION, and
the State of *Religion*.

III. *Relating* to the *Policy* and *Intereſts*
of ſome of the *States* of ITALY.

Being A SUPPLEMENT to Dr.
BURNETS LETTERS.

Printed in the Year 1688.

A TABLE

Of the *Contents* of the *Three*

LETTERS.

The first Letter.

Triple

The CONTENTS.

The CONTENTS.

† 3

The CONTENTS.

* 4

The CONTENTS.

The Second LETTER.

The CONTENTS.

The CONTENTS.

conducts

The CONTENTS.

The CONTENTS.

The CONTENTS.

The Third LETTER.

Im-

The CONTENTS.

The CONTENTS.

The CONTENTS.

The Stationer to the Reader.

I Can give no other account of these *Letters*, but that they were communicated to me, by a person of known Integrity ; who assured me, that he who made these *Observations*, is a man of great vertue, and considerably learned : who has been long and much in *Italy* : who is both capable of looking narrowly into matters, and is of such severe morals, that one may safely depend on all he says. This was enough for me ; so without making any further enquiry, or knowing any thing of the *Author*, I have set about the printing of them. VALE.

A

A
LETTER

Writ from

R · O · M · E,

To one in *Holland*, concerning the

QUIETISTS.

SIR,

Our defire of being informed particularly by me, of the ftate of *Religion* and *Learning* in *Italy*, and chiefly here at *Rome*, has quickned my curiofity, and has fet an edge upon a humour that is of it felf Inquifitive enough : and tho I am not fo much in love with writing, as to delight in tranfmitting you long *Letters*, yet I find I have matter at prefent for a very long one; chiefly in that which relates to the *Quietifts*: for you obferve right, that the fhort hints that **Dr. Burnet** gave of their matters in his *Letters*, did rather increafe the curiofity of the *English*, than fatisfy it. He told as much as was generally known in *Rome* at that time, concerning them; but as a longer ftay might have difcovered more particulars to him, fo there have fallen out fince that time fuch new and furprifing accidents, that there is not more hearkning after new *Evidence* in *England*, upon the breaking out of *Plots*, than there was at *Rome* upon the Imprifonment of fo great a number of perfons in *February* and *March* laft; the number alone of 200 *perfons*, was enough to raife a great curiofity; but this was much encreafed by the quality of the perfons that were clapt up, who were both for Rank, for Learning, and for Piety, the moft efteemed of any in *Rome*. So I was pufht on by my own Inclinations, as well as by your Entreaties, to take all the pains that was poffible for me, to be well Informed of this matter. The particular Application with which I had read fome of the Books of Devotion writ in this method, and the pleafure, and, I hope, profit, that I had found in it, made me ftill the more earneft to know this matter to the bottom. It is true, it was hard to find it out: for thofe who have been in *Rome*, know with how much caution all people there talk of matters that are before the *Inquifition*: thofe are like the Secrets of ftate elfewhere: of which a man cannot talk much without in-

incurring some Inconvenience; and there is no Inconvenience that is more terrible at *Rome*, than the falling into the hands of the *Inquisitors*: for besides the Danger that a man runs, if the suspitions are well founded, the least ill effect that this must have, is the cutting off all a mans hopes of Preferment; for what a Suspition of *High Treason* is elsewhere, the Suspition of *Heresy* is at *Rome*; and where there are many Pretenders, and there is so much to be expected, you may imagine that Hope and Fear working at the same time so powerfully, it must be very hard to ingage such persons as probably know the secret of things, to trust themselves upon so tender a point, to strangers.   The truth is, *Learning* is so low in *Italy*, and the Opinion that they have of the Learning of *Strangers*, chiefly of *Hereticks*, is so high, that they do not willingly enter either on Subjects of *Learning* or of *Religion* with them; and on the other hand a *Stranger* and a *Heretick*, who is considered as a *Spye*, or a fair Enemy at best, will not find it convenient to thrust on such subjects of conversation, as are tender and suspitious.   All this is to prepare you for a relation which you will perhaps think defective, yet is as full a I could possibly gather, out of all the Hints and Informations that some moneths stay at *Rome* procured me.

A 2   The

The firſt thing that ſurpriſes a *ſtranger* in *Rome*, is the very unequal mixture of *Wealth* and *Poverty*, that he ſees here, as well as in all the parts of *Italy*; yet it is more conſpicuous here, than elſewhere: for as the *Wealth* of the *Churches*, *Palaces* and *Convents* is aſtoniſhing, ſo the *Poverty* of the *Inhabitants*, and the meanneſs of the ordinary Buildings, is extremely unſuteable to the magnificence of the other. When a man ſees what *Italy* was an Age or two ago, not to go back ſo far as to remember what *Rome* was once; he can hardly imagin how ſuch a fall, ſuch a diſpeopling, and ſuch a poverty could befall a *Nation* and *Climate*, that Nature has made to be one of the richeſt of the world, or of *Europe* at leaſt; if the PRIESTS had not at the ſame time a ſecret to make the *Natives* miſerable, in ſpite of all that Abundance with which Nature has furniſhed them. It were not able to withſtand even an ordinary Enemy, and it can ſcarce ſupport it ſelf. Thoſe *Italians* that have ſeen the Wealth and Abundance that is in *England* and *Holland*, tho their *Sun* is leſs favorable, and their *Climate* is more unhappy, and that come home ſo ſee their *Towns* deſerted; and their *Inhabitants* in Raggs, ſpeak of this ſometimes with an Indignation that is too ſenſible to be at all times kept within bounds. They ſpeak of the difference between *Holland* and

Italy, like men affected when they compared the *two* foils and Climates together. The one is a *foil* divided between *fand* and *turff*, preferved from the Innudations of *Land-floods*, and the overflowing of the *fea*, at a vaft Charge, fuffering often fuch loffes as would ruin other *ftates*, and paying great and conftant Impofitions : and yet with all thefe Inconveniences, and all the difadvantages of a feeble *fun*, a ftagnating and phlegmatick *Air*, violent *Colds*, and moderate, or at leaft very fhorts *Heats*, this *Countrey* is full of *Wealth* and *People*; and there is in it fuch an abundance of great *Towns* and confiderable *villages*, and in all thefe there appear fo many marks of *plenty*, and none at all of *Want* : and the *other* has a kind *fun*, long and happy *Summers*, and mild *Winters* : a fruitful and rich *foil*, and every thing that the *Inhabitants* can wifh for on Natures part, to render them the Envy of the World : whereas they are become the *Scorn* and contempt of all that fee them. And as much as the *Dutch* feem to have acted in fpite of Nature on the one hand, in rendring themfelves much more confiderable than fhe has Intended they fhould be; fo the Government of *Italy* feems to have reverfed the defign of Nature as much on the other hand, by reducing the *Inhabitants* to fuch a degree of Mifery, in fpite of all her Bounty: upon this fubject

A 3   the

the *Italians* will talk more freely than upon matters of *Religion*: and do not stick to say, that it flows from the share that PRIESTS have in the Government, and that not only in the *Popes* Territory, but in all the other *Courts* of *Italy*, where they have the main stroke. They will tell you, that *Priests* have not Souls big enough, nor tender enough, for Government: they have both a narrowness of spirit, and a sourness of mind, that does not agree with the Principles of human Society : Their having so short and so uncertain a time of governing, makes them think only on the present, so that they do not carry their prospect to the Happiness of, or misery that must be the consequences of what they do, at any considerable distance of time: nor have they those Compassions for the Miserable with which wise *Governours* ought to temper all their Counsells; for a stern sourness of temper, and an unrelenting hardness of heart, seems to belong to all that sort of *men* in *Italy*. Whatsoever advances their present Interests, and inriches their families, is preferred to all wise, great or generous councells. Now tho the *Natives* dare not carry this matter further, yet a *stranger*, that thinks more freely, and that has examined matters of Religion, in a more Inquisitive manner, sees plainly that all these errors in *Government*, are the effects

effects of their *Religion*, and of that authority which they believe is lodged in the *Pope*,
chiefly and of which every *Prieſt* has ſo conſiderable a ſhare , that he is eaſily able to
make himſelf maſter of every mans Conſci-
ence that lets him into it , and that believes
thoſe *three* great branches of their power :
that *they can pardon their ſins* , *make their
God*, and *ſecure them both from Hell and Purgatory.* Theſe are things of ſuch a mighty
operation, that if it is not eaſy to imagine how
they ſhould be ſo eaſily believed, yet ſuppo-
ſing once the belief of them , all other
things flow very naturally from thence : men
are not convinced of theſe errors till it is too
late to come and undeceive others. It is true,
many of the *Italians* believe theſe things
as little as we do ; yet this is in them rather
an effect of a looſe and libertine temper, than
of ſtudy and enquiry , in a *Countrey* where
not only *Heretical books* would endanger a
man, but the bare reading even of a *Latin*
New *Teſtament* would give ſome ſuſpition.
But the thinking men among them are led to
doubt of all things, rather from a principle of
Atheiſm, than of ſearching into matters of
Controverſy : the one is much leſs dangerous
there, than the other would be. And indeed
as ſoon as a man becomes a little familiar with
any of the *men* of freer thoughts here, he will
ſoon ſee that the belief of their *Religion* has
A 4   ver y

very little power over many of those who are the most zealous to support it, only because their Interest determins them. When a man has lived some time at *Rome*, and has known a little of the Mysteries of the *Conclave*, with the *Character* both of the present and the late *Popes*, particularly the weakness and Ignorance of *him*, that now *reigns*, who does not so much as understand *Latin*; when a man sees how matters are carried in that *Court*, what are the *Maximes* they go by, and the *Methods* that they take; when he sees what a sort of men the *Cardinals* are, men indeed of great Civility, and of much Craft; but as to the matters of *Religion*, men of an equal size both of Ignorance and Indifference: when a man sees how all preferments are obtained, but chiefly how the *purple* is given, and how men rise up to the *Triple Crown*: when, I say, a man has seen and observed all this a little, he cannot wonder enough at the *Character* that so great a part of the World sets on that *Court*. The plain and simple Arguments of Common sense work so strong, that *Transubstantiation* it self is not harder to be believed, than that this man is Christs *Vicar*, a man of *Infallibility*, and the source or channel at least of divine *truth*. So that a man that has given himself the opportunities of observing these matters Critically, will feel a persuasion of the falsehood of those pretensions formed so deep in him, that all the Sophi-

ftry

ftry of Argument will never be able to over-
throw it: for the plain fenfe of what he has
feen will apparently difcover the delufion of
thofe Reafons, which perhaps he is not learned enough to anfwer: for let men fay what
they will, it is no eafy matter to believe in a
Contradiction to the clear Evidence of fence:
and I cannot make my felf fo much as doubt,
but that as *Cato* was wont to wonder how it
came that every one of the *Heathen Priefts* did
not laugh when he faw another of the *Trade*, fo
the *Cardinals* when they look on one another,
and a *Pope* even as Ignorant a one as the *prefent
Pope* is, when he receives the fubmiffions that
are offered him by all who are of that *Communion*, muft laugh within himfelf when he
fees how lucky that Impofture is, which has
fubdued the World into fo much refpect for
him, and to fo great a dependance on him.
A *man* who fees all thefe things upon the place,
and is of an Age capable of making folid
Reflections, and has a due portion of Learning, muft return amafed, not fo much at thofe
who being already under the *Yoke*, have neither knowledge nor courage enough to fhake
it off, nor at thofe who go into it becaufe they
find their account in it, and fo hope to have a
good fhare of the fpoil, as at *thofe* who have
fhaken off the Yoke, and have got into more
Liberty and more *Knowledg*, and feel the happy Influence of their deliverance even in their

A 5   *Civil*

Civil Liberties and other *Temporal* Concerns, if they should ever come so much as to delibe-rate whether they ought to return and serve their old and severe *Masters*, or not.   For my part, I speak freely to you, that I could sooner bring my mind to believe that there is no such thing as *Instituted Religion*; and that it is enough for men to be just and honest, civil and obliging, and to have a general re-verence for the *Deity*, than ever to think that such *Stuff* as the *men* of the *Mission* would im-pose on the World can be true.   Chiefly in that part of it which relates to the *Popes Authority*, after all that I have seen and known.

You will perhaps think, that this is a long digression, or at least a very improper intro-duction to that which I told you I would offer to you, since the relation that all this has with the matter of the *Quietists*, does not appear to be so very proper.   Yet you will perhaps change your mind, when I tell you, that the Miseries of *Italy*, that the Aversion that all men of sense there have to the Ar-tifices of their *Religion*, and chiefly to the conduct of the *Regulars*, and above all, of the *Jesuites*, is believed the true reason that led such numbers of *men* of all sorts to be so favourable to *Molinos* : to which this was rather to be ascribed, than to any Extraordi-nary Elevation of Piety or Devotion, of which fo little appears in that Country, that nothing which touches only upon that Principle can have great effects among them.   Men that are fick, turn to all forts of remedies : and thofe who are difcontented, do naturally go into every new thing that either promifes relief, or that wounds thofe that difpleafe them. The prefent ftate of things in *Italy* being fuch as I have defcribed it, you need not wonder to find fo many ready to hearken after any thing that feemed both *new* and *fafe*.   For as the Novelty gave that curiofity which might draw in many, fo the fafety that feemed to be in a Method of Devotion in which fo many of the Canonifed *Saints* had gone before them, and which appeared at firft authorifed by the Approbation of fo many *Inquifitours*, made them apprehend that there could be no danger in it.   In the recital that I am to give you, I do not pretend to tell you all the whole affair : nor will I affure you of the truth of all that you will find here.   For in matters of this nature, in which Intereft and Paffion are apt to work fo ftrongly, there are alwayes fo many falfe Reports fpread, and matters are fo often aggravated on the one hand, and diminifhed or denied on the other, that I will not fay but there may be fome things here that upon a ftricter inquiry will perhaps appear not to be well founded ; yet of this I will affure

you

you very positively, that I have Invented
and added nothing my self. I leave those
arts to the *Italians*, and the *Court* of *Rome*:
therefore I will tell you things nakedly
and simply, as I found them, without adding
so much as one Circumstance out of my
own Invention. I also made as much use
of my Judgment as was possible for me to do,
both in considering theCircumstances of those
with whom I talked on those heads, and the
things themselves that they said to me; so I let
pass all that seemed to be the effect of Passion or Prejudice, and only marked down
that which seemed to be true, as well as that
which I had from men whom I had reason to
believe. My *Informers* were men of Pro-
bity and of Sense; they were not indeed easily brought to talk of this *Subject*, and they
spoke of it with great Reserves : so that
there may be many defects, and possibly
some mistakes in the account that I am to offer
you; yet you must be contented with it;
for it is all that I could gather ; and it is
not corrupted with any mixture of my
own.

    Michael de Molinos is a *Spaniard*, of a
good and Opulent Family. He entred into
Priests Orders, but had never any Ecclesiastical *Benefice*: so that he seemed to have dedicated himself to the service of the *Church*,
without designing any Advantage by it to
him-

himfelf. He paffes in *Italy* for a man both
of *Learning* and of good *Senfe*. His courfe
of life has been exact, but he has never practifed thofe Aufterities that are fo much magnified in the *Church* of *Rome*, and among the
Religious *Orders*: and as he did not affect to
practife them, fo he did not recommend
them to others ; nor was he fond of thofe
poor *Superftitions* that are fo much magnified by the trafficking men of that *Church*
But he gave in to the Method of the *Myftical.*
Divines, of which, fince your ftudies have
not perhaps lien much that way, I fhall give
you this fhort account.

That fublime, but myfterious way of *De-*
votion, was not fet out by any of the firft
Writers of the *Church* ; which is indeed a
great Prejudice againft it : for how many
foever they may be, who have followed it in
the latter Ages , yet *Caffians Collations*,
which is a work of the midle of the *fifth*
Century , is the antienteft Book that is writ
in that ftrain : for the pretended *Denis* the
Areopagite is now by the confent of all learned
men thought no Elder than the end of the
fifth or the beginning of the fixth Century.
Yet after thefe *Books* appeared , very few
followed the elevated ftrains that were in
them : the latter was indeed too dark to be
either well underftood or much followed. So
that this way of *Devotion*, if it was practifed
in

in *Religious Houses*, yet was not much set out to the World before S. *Bernards* time, whose melting strains, tho a little too much laboured and affected, yet have something in them that both touches and pleases : after him many began to write in that sublime strain; such as *Thauler*, *Rusbrachius*, *Harphius*, *Suso*, but above all *Thomas a Kempis*. And when for some considerable time that way of *writing* was discontinued, it was again raised up in the last Age, with much luster by S. *Teresa*; and after her by *Baltasar Alvares* a *Jesuit*: and as *England* produced a *Carthusian* in King *Henry* the sixths time, one *Walter Hilton*, who writ the *Scale of Perfection*; a Book Inferior to none of these I have cited, and more simple and natural than most of them; so of late F. *Cressy* has published out of F. *Bakers* Papers, who was a *Benedictine*, a whole body of that method of *Divinity* and *Devotion*. The right notion of this way of Devotion is somewhat hard to be well understood, by those who have not studied their *Metaphisicks*, and is entangled with too many of the terms of the School; yet I shall give it to you as free of these as is possible.

With relation to *Devotion* they consider a man in *three* different degrees of Progress and Improvement : the first is the *Animal*, or the Imaginative state : in which the Im-
pres-

preffions of *Religion* work ftrongly upon a
mans Fancy, and his fenfitive Powers : this
ftate is but low and mean, and futeable to
the Age of a Child; and all the *Devotion* that
works this way, that raifes a heat in the
Brain, tendernefs in the Thoughts, that
draws Sighs and Tears, and that awakens many melting *Imaginations,* is of a low form, va-
riable, and of no great force.   The fecond
ftate is the *Rational*, in which thofe Reflections that are made on Truths, which convince ones *reafon*, carry one to all futeable
Acts : this they fay is dry, and without mo-
tion : it is a Force which the Reafon puts
upon the Will, and tho upon a great Variety
of Motives, and many *Meditations* upon
them, the mind goes thro a great many
Performances of *Devotion*, yet this is ftill a
Force put upon the *will.* So they reckon
that the third and higheft ftate is the *Contemplative*, in which the *Will* is fo united to
God, and overcome by that Union, that in
one fingle Act of *Contemplation*, it adores
God, it loves him, and refigns it felf up to
him : and without wearying it felf with a dry
multiplicity *of Acts,* it feels in one Act of Faith
more force than a whole day of Meditation
can produce.   In this they fay that a true *Contemplative Man*, feels a fecret Ioy in God,
and an acquiefcing in his Will; in which the
true elevation of *Devotion* lies; and which is
far

far above either the heats of *Fancy*, which accompany the *first* state, or the Subtilty of *Meditation*, that belongs to the *second* state : and
they say, that the perfection of a *Contemplative
state* above the others, appears in this, that
wheras all men are not capable of forming
lively *Imaginations*, or of a fruitful Invention,
yet every man is capable of the simplicity of
contemplation : which is nothing *but the silent
and humble adoration of God, that arises out of
a pure and quiet mind*. But because all this
may appear a little Intricate, I shall illustratte
it by a similitude, which will make the difference of those *three states* more sensible;1.A *man*
that sees the exteriour of *another*, with whom
he has no acquaintance, and is much taken
with his face, shape, quality, and meen,
and this has a blind prevention in his favour,
and a sort of a feeble kindness for him, may be
compared to him whose *Devotion* consists in
lively *Imaginations*, and tender Impressions
on his lower and sensible Powers: 2. A *man*
that upon an acquaintance with *another*,
sees a great many reasons to value and esteem,
both his parts and his Vertues, yet in all
this he feels no inward Charm that over-
comes him, and knits his soul to the other;
so that how high soever the esteem may be, yet
it is cold and dry, and does not affect his
heart much, may be compared to one whose
Devotion consists in many Acts, and much
Me-

Meditation. But 3dly, when a *man* enters into an entire friendship with *another*, then one single Thought of his Friend, affects him more tenderly, than all that variety of reflections, which may arise in his mind, where this Union is not felt. And thus they explain the sublime state of *Contemplation.* And they reckon that all the common methods of *Devotion*, ought to be considered, only as steps to raise men up to this state: when men rest and continue in them, they are but dead and lifeless Forms: and if they rise above them, they become Cloggs and Hindrances, which amuse them with many dry Performances, in which those who are of a higher Dispensation will feel no pleasure nor advantage. Therefore the use of the *Rosary*, the daily repeating the *Breviary*, together with the common *Devotions* to the *Saints*, are generally laid aside by those who rise up to the *Contemplative* State; and the chief business to which they apply themselves, is *to keep their Minds in an inward Calm and Quiet*, that so they may in silence form simple *Acts* of Faith, and feel those *inward Motions* and *Directions* which they believe follow all those who rise up to this Elevation. But because a man may be much deceived in those Inspirations, therefore they recommend to all who enter into this method, above all other things, the choice of a *Spiritual Guide*,

B who

who has a right fenfe and a true taft of thofe
matters, and is by Confequence a Competent
Judge in them.

This is all that I will lay before you in general, for giving you fome taft of *Molinos's* Methods; and by this you will both
fee why his *Followers* are called Q U I E-
T I S T S and why his *Book* is Entitled *il Gui-
da Spirituale.* But if you Intend to Inform
your felf more particularly of this matter,
you muft feek for it, either in the *Authors*
that I have already mentioned, or in thofe of
which I am to give you fome account in the
fequel of this Letter. *Molinos* having it
feems drunk in the principles of the **Contemplative Devotion** in *Spain* , where the great
Veneration that is payed to S. *Terefa* gives
it much reputation , he brought over with
him to *Italy* a great Zeal for propagating it.
He came and fetled at *Rome* , where he writ
his *Book,* and entred into a great commerce
with the *men* of the beft Apprehenfions, and
the moft Elevated thoughts that he found
there. All that feemed to concur with him
in his defign for fetting on foot this fublimer
way , were not perhaps animated with the
fame principles. Some defigned fincerly to
elevate the World above thofe poor and trif-
ling *Superftitions* , that are fo much in vogue,
among all the *Bigots* of the Church of *Rome*,
but more particularly in *Spain* and *Italy* , and
which

which are so much set on by almost all the *Regulars*, who seem to place *Religion* chiefly in the exact performing of them.   It was thought that others entred into the design upon more Indirect motives. Some perhaps from the aversion that they bore the *Regulars*, were disposed to entertain every thing that might lead mens *Devotions* into other Channells, and to a conduct different from that prescribed by *Friers* and *Jesuites*.   Some perhaps had understandings good enough to see the necessity of correcting many things in their Worship, which yet they durst not attack as simply unlawful :   so that it might appear more safe to expose these things to the Contempt of the World , by pretending to raise men far above them: and thus they might have hoped to have Introduced a *Reformation* of many Abuses without seeming to do it.   *In fine,* some who seemed to enter into this matter , were men that aspired to fame , and hoped by this means to raise a Name to themselves ; and to have a Party that should depend upon them: for in such great numbers as seemed to imbark in this design, it is not to be imagined that all were acted by the same motives , and that every man had as good Intentions as it is probable *Molinos* himself had.

In the year 1675. his *Book* was first published with *five Approbations* before it. One

B 2   of

of thefe was by the *Archbishop* of *Rheggio*;
another was by the *General* of the *Francifcans*,
who was likewife one of the *Qualificators* of
the *Inquifition*: another was by Fa. *Martin de
Efparfa* a Jefuit, that had been Divinity *Pro-
feffor* both at *Salamanca* and at *Rome*; and was
at that time a *Qualificator of the Inquifition.*
As for the reft, I refer you to the *Book* it felf.
The *Book* was no fooner printed, than it was
much read and highly efteemed both in *Italy*
and *Spain*. It was confidered as a *Book* writ
with much Clearnefs and great fimplicity; and
this fo raifed the Reputation of the *Author*,
that his Acquaintance came to be generally
much defired: thofe who were in the greateft
credit in *Rome*, feemed to value themfelves
upon his friendfhip. *Letters* were writ to
him from all places: fo that a correfpondence
was fetled between him and thofe who approved of his *method* in many different places of
Europe. Some fecular *Priefts* both at *Rome*
and *Naples* declared themfelves openly for it:
and confulted him as a fort of an Oracle upon
many occafions. But thofe who joyned themfelves to him with the greateft Heartinefs and
Sincerity, were fome of the *Fathers* of the *Ora-
tory*, in particular *three* of the moft Eminent
of them, who were all advanced at the laft
promotion of Cardinals, *Coloredi*, *Ciceri*, but
above all *Petrucci*, who was accounted his
Timothy. Many of the *Cardinals* were alfo
ob-

obferved to court his Acquaintance : and they
thought it no fmall Honour to be reckoned in
the number of *Molinos's* Friends. Such were
Caffanata Azolini and *Carpegna* ; but above
all Card. *d'Eftrees*. The laft you muft needs
know, is a man of great Learning : he was Am-
bitious to be thought a *Reformer* of fome of
thofe Abufes, which are among them, that
are too grofs to pafs upon a man of his freedom
of fpirit ; who had been bred up in the *Sorbon*,
and had converfed much with Mr. de *Launay*.
He therefore feemed the moft zealous of all
others to advance *Molinos's* Defign : fo that he
entered into a very clofe commerce with him.
They were oft and long together : and notwithftanding all the diftruft that a *Spaniard*
has naturally of a *Frenchman* , and that all
men have of one another, who have lived long
at *Rome*, yet *Molinos*, who was fincere and
plain-hearted, opened himfelf without referve
to the *Cardinal*: and by his means a Correfpondence was fetled between *Molinos* and
fome in *France*: for tho the fpirits of thofe of
that *Nation* go generally too quick for a way
of *Devotion*, that was fetled and filent, yet
fome were ftrongly Inclined to favour it even
there. Perhaps it might be confidered as a
method more like to gain upon *Proteftants*,
and to facilitate the Defign of the *Re-union*,
that was fo long talked of there. All thefe
things concurred to raife *Molinos's* Cha-

　　　　　racter,

racter, and to render his perfon
ble. When the *Pope* that now *rei*
vanced to the *Throne*, which wa
in the year 1676. that he took m
notice of him: and made it Vifib
that even in all thar. Exaltation
it might contribute to raife his
he were confidered as a friend of
an Encourager of his Defign: I
him in an Appartment of the *Pa*
many fingular Marks of his Ef
This made him become ftill th
fpicuous, when he had the adva
vour joyned to his other Qualitie
ther feemed to be fond of it, nor
it.   His Converfation was muc
many *Priefts* came not only t
felves according to his *Method*,
all their Penetents to follow it
to be fo much in vogue in *Ron*
Nuns, except thofe who had *P*
Confeffors, began to lay afide the
other *Devotions*, and to give the
to the practice of *Mental prayer*
more Credit given to it by the t
French Book, that was writ i
fubject, which Cardinal *d'Ef*
be made. It was writ in the form
and was printed in *France* in the
the *Approbation* of fome of th
the *Sorbon*. I am able to give yo

count of the *Author*, but that in the *Italian* Tranflation he is called *Francis Mallevalla*, a blind Clergy-man. The *Book* being chiefly formed upon the model of *S. Terefe*, the Tranflation of it was dedicated to the *Difcalçiate Carmelites* of her Order. This did not contribute a little for raifing the credit of *Molinos's Method*, fince it appeared to be approved both in *Italy*, *France* and *Spain*. At the fame time *Fa. Petrucci* writ a great many *Letters* and *Treatifes* relating to a *Contemplative State* : yet he mixed in many of them, fo many Rules relating to the *Devotions* of the *Quire*, that there was lefs occafion given for cenfure in his *Writings* : They are a little too tedious ; but they were writ chiefly for *Nuns* and others, that perhaps could not have apprehended his meaning aright, if he had exprefled himfelf in a clofer ftile, and in fewer words. Both the *Jefuites* and the *Dominicans* began to be alarmed at the progrefs of *Quietifm:* they faw clearly, that their trade was in a decay, and muft decay ftill more and more, if fome ftop was not put to the progrefs of this *new Method* : in order to this, is was neceffary to decry the *Authors* of it: and becaufe of all the Imputations in the world *Herefy* is that, which makes the greateft Impreffion at *Rome*, *Molinos* and his *Followers* were given out to be *Hereticks*. It being alfo neceffary to faften a particular

Name

Name to every *new Heresy*, they branded this with the Name of <u>*Quietism*</u>. Books were also writ by some *Jesuites* against *Molinos* and his Method; in which there appeared much of that Sourness and Malignity that is thought to be peculiar to the *Society*; they were also writ with their usual candor and sincerity. One of the Fathers *Segueri* took a more dextrous Method to decry it. He began his Book magnifying the *Contemplative State* highly, as Superiour to all others; and blaming those who had said any. thing that seemed to detract from it: yet he corrected all this, by saying, *that very few were capable of it*; and *that none ought to pretend to it, but those who were called by God to so sublime a State:* and by this he seemed only to censure the Indiscretion of those *Spiritual Guides*, who proposed this way of *Devotion* to all persons, without distinction. He also believed, that such as were at some times called to it, could not remain long in so high a state, to which God called men rather for some happy Minutes, than for a longer continuance: therefore he thought that such persons as were raised to it, ought not to fancy that they were now got so far above all their former helps, as never to need them any more: so he proposed to them the accustoming themselves still to *Meditation*, and to support themselves by that when they could not

con-

contemplate. He cenfured feverely fome of *Molinos's* expreffions, fuch as that, *He who had God, had Chrift* ; as if this were an abandoning of Chrifts Humanity : he alfo infifted much on that of *a fixed looking on God*, and the *fuſpending of all the Powers of the Soul*: but that on which he infifted moſt, was that *Molinos* (whom he never named, tho he cited his Words, and defcribed him very plainly) made the Quiet of *Contemplation* to be a *State* to which a man could raife himfelf; whereas he maintains, that in this Quiet the *Soul* is *paſſive*, and as it were in a rapture ; and that fhe could not raife her felf to it, but that it was an Immediat and Extraordinary Favour, which was only to be expected from God, and which an humble mind could not fo much as aſk of him.

Thefe Difputes raifed fo much noife in *Rome*, that the *Inquifition* took *Notice* of the whole matter : *Molinos* and his *Book*, and *F. Petrucci's Treatiſes* and *Letters*, were brought under a fecond and feverer Examination ; and here the *Jefuites* were confidered as the Accufers. It is true, one of the *Society*, as was formerly told, had approved *Molinos*'s Book ; but they took care that he fhould be no more feen at *Rome*: for he was fent away, and it is not known whether, it is generally believed that he is fhut up within *Four Walls*; but what truth foever may be in

B 5   that

that, he is no more visible, so careful are they to have all their *Order* speak the same Language; and if any speak in a different stile from the rest, they at least take care that he shall speak no more; yet in this *Examen* that was made, both *Molinos* and *Petrucci* justified themselves so well, that their Books were again approved, and the Answers which the *Iesuites* had writ, were censured as scandalous: and in this matter *Petrucci* behaved himself so signally well, that it raised not only the Credit of the Cause, but his own Reputation so much, that soon after he was made *Bishop* of *Iessi*, which was a new Declaration that the *Pope* made in their Favours: their *Books* were now more esteemed than ever, their Method was more followed, and the Novelty of it, the opposition made to it, by a *Society* that has rendred it self odious to all the World, and the new *Approbation* that was given to it after so vigorous an Accusation, did all contribute to raise the Credit and to encrease the Numbers of the Party. *F. Petrucci's* behaviour in his *Bishoprick*, contributed to raise his Reputation still higher, so that his Enemy's were willing to give him no more Disturbance; and indeed there was less occasion given for Censure by his *Writings*, than by *Molino's* little *Book*; whose succinctness made that some Passages were not so fully nor so cautiously expressed,

but

but that there was room for making Exceptions to them: on the other hand, *Petrucci* was rather exceffively tedious, fo that he had fo fully explained himfelf, that he very eafily cleared fome fmall difficulties that were made upon fome of his *Letters:* In fhort, every body was that thought either fincerely devout, or that at leaft affected the Reputation of it, came to be reckoned among the *Quietifts:* and if thefe perfons were obferved to become more ftrict in their *Lives*, more retired and ferious in their mental *Devotions*, yet there appeared lefs *Zeal* in their whole deportment as to the exteriour parts of the *Religion* of that *Church*. They were not fo affiduous at *Mafs*, nor fo earneft to procure *Maffes* to be faid for their Friends: nor were they fo frequently either at *Confeffion* or in *Proceffions:* fo that the Trade of thofe that live by thefe things was fenfibly funk : and tho the new *Approbation* that was given to *Molinos's Book* by the *Inquifition* ftopt the Mouths of his Enemies, fo that they could no more complain of it, yet they did not ceafe to fcatter about Surmifes of all that fort of men, as of a *Cabale*, that would have dangerous confequences; they remembred the ftory of the *Illuminated Men* of *Spain*, and faid, here was a Spawn of the fame Sect: they infinuated, that they had ill Defigns, and profound Secrets among them; that thefe were in their

Hearts

Hearts Enemies to the *Christian Religion*; and that under a pretence of raising men to a most sublime strain of *Devotion*, they intended to wear out of their minds the sense of the Death and Sacrifice of *Christ*, and of the other Mysteries of *Christianity*: and because *Molinos* was by his birth a *Spaniard*, it has been given out of late, that perhaps he was descended of a *Jewish* or *Mahometan* Race, and that he might carry in his Blood, or in his first Education, some Seeds of those *Religions*, which he has since cultivated, with no less Art than Zeal: yet this last Calumny has gained but little Credit at *Rome*; tho it is said, that an Order has been sent to examine the Registers of the Baptism, in the place of his Birth, to see if his Name is to be found in it or not.

Thus he saw himself attacked with great vigour, and with an unrelenting Malice. He took as much care as was possible to prevent, or to shake off these Imputations; for he writ a Treatise, of *frequent and dayly Communion*, which was likewise approved by some of the most learned of the *Regulars* at *Rome*, among whom one is *Martinez* a *Jesuite*, the Senior *Divinity Reader* in their Colledge at *Rome*. This was printed with his *Spiritual Guide*, in the year 1675. and in the *Preface* he protests, that he had not writ it with any design to engage himself into matters

ters of Controverſy, but that it was drawn from him, by the moſt earneſt Solicitations of ſome Zealous Perſons.   In it he preſſed a *daily Communion*, by a vaſt number of Paſ-ſages that he cited both out of the Ancient *Fathers*, and the *Schoolmen*; yet he qualified this and all his other directions in the matters of *Devotion* by that which he conſtantly re-peats, which is the neceſſity of being con-ducted in all things by a *Spiritual Guide* : whe-ther he intended to ſoften the averſion that the *Jeſuites* had to him, by refuting ſome parts of Mr. *Arnaud's* famous Book of *Frequent Communion* or not, I cannot tell, but in this Diſcourſe he anſwers ſome of the Ob-jections that Mr. *Arnaud* had made to *Frequent Communion*, and in particular, to that which he makes one main ground of reſtrai-ning men from it, which was the obliging them to go thro with their Penitence and Mor-tifications, before they were admitted to the *Sacrament* ; whereas *Molinos* makes the being free of *Mortal Sin*, the only neceſſary qualification. In this Diſcourſe one ſees more of a heated Eloquence, than of ſevere or ſo-lid Reaſoning : yet it preſſes the point of *daily Communion*, and of *an inward applica-tion of Soul to Ieſus Chriſt, and to his Death*, ſo vehemently, that it might have been ho-ped that this ſhould have put an end to thoſe Surmiſes, that had been thrown out to de-

fame

fame him ; as if he had defigned to lay afide
the Humanity of our Saviour, by his way
of *Devotion* : but there is no cure for Jea-
louſy ; eſpecially when Malice and Intereſt
are at bottom : ſo new matter was found for
cenſure in this Diſcourſe. He had aſſerted,
that there was no other Preparation neceſſary,
but to be free of *Mortal Sin* : ſo it was given
out, that he intended to lay afide *Confeſſion* :
and tho he had adviſed the uſe of a *Spiritual
Guide*, in this, as well as in all other things ;
yet the neceſſity of *Confeſſion* before *Communion*, was not expreſſed : ſo that by this people ſeemed to be ſet at Liberty from that Obli-
gation : and it was ſaid, that what he adviſed
with relation to a *Spiritual Guide*, lookt rather like the taking ſome general Directions
and Council from ones *Prieſt*, than the coming alwayes to him as the *Miniſter* of the
Sacrament of *Pennance* before every *Communion* ; and to ſupport this Imputation, it
was ſaid, that all of that *Cabale* had ſet
down this for a Rule, by which they con-
ducted their Penitents, that they might come
to the Sacrament, when they found themſelves
out of the ſtate of *Mortal ſin*, without going
at every time to *Confeſſion* ; but I will not inlarge further upon the matters of *Doctrine* or
Devotion, in which you may think that I
have dwelt too long, for a man of my Breeding and Profeſſion : and I ſhould think ſo
                                            my

my felf, if I were not confining my felf exactly to the *Memorials* and *Informations* that
I received at *Rome*. You will fee by the *Articles* objected to the *Quietifts*, and cenfured
by one of the *Inquifition*, which I fend you
with this *Letter*, what are all the other
points that are laid to their charge. Only I
muft advertife you of one thing, that their
Friends at *Rome* fay, that a great many of
thefe *Articles* are only the Calumnies of their
Enemies, and that they are difowned by
them: but that they have faftned thefe things
on them, to render them odious, and to
make them fuffer with the lefs Pitty: which
is the putting in practice the fame Maximes
which we object to their Predeceffors, who
condemned the *Waldenfes* and *Albigenfes* of a
great many Errors of which they alwayes
protefted themfelves Innocent: yet the Ac-
cufing them of thofe horrid Opinions and
Practices, prevailed upon the Simplicity and
Credulity of the Age, to animate them with
all the Degrees of Rage againft a Sect of men,
that were fet forth as Monfters: the fame
Maximes and Politicks are ftill imputed, and
perhaps not without reafon to that fevere
Court, which if you believe many has as
little regard to Juftice as it has to Mercy.
Some have carried their Jealoufies fo far a-
gainft the *Quietifts*, as to compare their
Maxims to thofe of *Socrates* his *School*, and
· his

his *Followers* after his death, when they faw what his Freedom in fpeaking openly againft the eftablifht *Religion* had coft him: they refolved to comply with the received Cuftoms in their exteriour, and not to communicate their *Philofophy* to the Vulgar; nor even to their Difciples, till they had prepared them well to it, by training them long in the precepts of *Vertue*, which they called the *Purgative State*: and when men were well tried and exercifed in this, then they communicated to them their fublimer Secrets: the meaning of all which was, in fhort, that they would not difcover their Opinions in thofe points that were contrary to the received *Religion*, and to the publick *Rites* to any, but to thofe of whom they were well affured, that they would not betray them: and therefore they fatisfied themfelves with having true and juft notions of things; but they practifed outwardly as the Rabble did. They thought it was no great matter what Opinions were entertained by them, and that none but *men* of *Noble* and elevated Tempers deferved that fuch fublime Truths fhould be communicated to them, and that the herd of the *Vulgar* neither were worthy nor capable of Truth, which is too pure and too high a thing for fuch mean and bafe minds. The Affinity of the matter makes me remember a converfation that I once had with one of the wittieft

Clergy-

Clergy-men of *France*, who is likewise efteemed one of the *Learnedft Men* in it ; He faid,
*The World could not bear a Religion calculated
only for* Philofophers: *The people did not know
what it was to think, and to govern themfelves by
the Impreffions that abftracted thoughts made on
their minds: they muft have outward things to
ftrike upon their fenfes and Imaginations, to a-
mufe, to terrify and to excite them*: fo legends,
dreadful ftories *and a pompous* Worfhip *were
neceffary to make the Impreffions of* Religion *go
deep into fuch courfe fouls: for a Lancet*, faid
he, *can open a vein, but an Axe muft fell
down a Tree*; fo he concluded, *that the* Reformation *had reduced the* Chriftian Religion *to
fuch fevere terms, that among us it was only a*
Religion *for* Philofophers: *and fince few were
capable of that ftrength of thought*: he concluded, *that if the* Church of Rome *had perhaps
too much of this exteriour pomp, thofe of the* Reformation *had ftript it too much, and had not
left enough of garnifhing, and of the bells and
feathers for amufing the rable.* The fpeculation
feems pretty enough, if *Religion* were to be
confidered only as a contrivance of ours, to be
fitted by us to the tempers and humours of
People; and not as a Body of *Divine Truths*,
that are conveyed to us from heaven.

Thus was *Molinos's* method cenfured or
approved in *Rome*, according to the different
Apprehenfions and Interefts of thofe that
C
made

made Reflections upon it. But the *Jesuites* finding they were not so omnipotent in this *Pontificate*, as they have been formerly, resolved to carry their point another *way*. I need not tell you how great an Ascendant *F. la Chaise* has gained over that *Monarch*, that has been so long the *terrour of Europe:* and how much all the *Order* is now in the Interests of *France*. The *Zeal* with which that *King* has been extirpating *Heresy*, Furnishes them with abundance of matter for high *Panegyricks*; since that which in the opinion of many will pass down to posterity, for the lasting reproach of a *Reign*, which in its former parts has seemed to approach even to *Augustus's* Glory, but has received in this a stain, which with Indifferent men passes for a blind, poor-spirited and furious *Bigottry*, and is represented by *Protestants* as a complication of as much Treachery and Cruelty as the World ever saw ; yet among the *bigots* it is set forth as the brightest side of that Glorious *Reign*: and therefore it has been often cited by them with relation to the cold correspondence that is observed to be between the *Courts* of *Rome*, and that at *Versailles*, that nothing was more Incongruous, than to see the *Head of the Church* dispute so obstinatly with its *Eldest son* such a trifle, as the matter of the *Regale*, and that with so much eagerness ; and that he shew'd so little regard to so great a *Monarch*, that seemed to sacrifice
all

all his own *Interests* to thole of his *Religion* :
It is believed, that the *Jesuits* at *Rome*, propo-
ted the matter of *Molinos* to *F. la Chaise*, as a fit
reproach to be made to the *Pope*, in that *Kings*
name, that while he himself was Imploying
all possible means to extirpate *Heresy* out of his
Dominions. The *Pope* was cherishing it in his
own *Palace*: and that while the *Pope* pretended to such an unyielding *Zeal* for the *Rights*
of the *Church*, he was entertaining a person
who was corrupting the *doctrine*, or at least
the *devotion*, of that *Body*, of which he had
the honour to be the *Head.* But here I must
add a thing which comes very uneasily from
me, and yet I cannot keep my word to you,
of giving you a faithful account of all that I
could learn of this matter at *Rome*, without
mentioning it. I do not pretend to affirm it
is true, for I only tell you what is believed at
Rome, and not what I believe my self, nor
what I would have you to believe; for I know
you have so high an esteem of Cardinal *d'E-*
strees, that you will not easily believe any thing
that is to his Disadvantage. It is then said,
that *he* being commanded by the *Orders* that
were sent him from the *Court* of *France*, to
prosecute *Molinos* with all possible vigour, resolved to sacrifice his old *Friend*, and all that
is sacred in *Friendship*, to the Passion he has for
His Masters *Glory*; finding then that there
was not matter enough for an Accusation

C 2   against

againſt *Molinos*, he reſolved to ſupply that
defect himſelf; ſo that he, who was once as
deep as any man alive in the whole Secret of
this Affair, went and Informed the *Inquiſition*
of many particulars, for which tho there was
no other evidence but his Teſtimony, yet that
was ſufficient to raiſe a great Storm againſt
Molinos; and upon this delation, *he* and a
few others of his friends were put in the *Inquiſition*; but this was managed ſo ſecretly, that
all that is pretended to be known concerning
it, is, that upon a new Proſecution both *Molinos* and *Petrucci* were brought before the
Inquiſition in 1684. *Petrucci* was ſoon abſolved;
for there was ſo little objected to him, and he
anſwered that with ſo much Judgement and
Temper, that he was quickly diſmiſſed; and
tho *Molinos's* matter was longer in agitation,
yet is was generally expected that he ſhould
have been acquitted. In concluſion, a Correſpondence held by him all *Europe* over, was
objected to him: but that could be no Crime,
unleſs the matter of that Correſpondence
was Criminal : ſome ſuſpitions papers were
found in his Chamber, but as he himſelf explained them, nothing could be made out of
them, till Cardinal *d'Eſtrees* delivered a *Letter* and a *Meſſage* from the *King* of *France* to
the *Pope*, as was formerly mentioned : and
that the *Cardinal* added, that he himſelf could
prove againſt *Molinos*, more than was neceſſary

ceſſary to ſhew that he was guilty of *Hereſy*. The *Pope* ſaid not a word to this , but left the matter to the *Inquiſitors*; and the *Cardinal* went to them , and gave other ſenſes of thoſe doubtful Paſſages , that were in *Molinos's Books* and *Papers*, and pretended that he knew from himſelf, what his true Meaning in them was. The *Cardinal* owned, that he had lived with him in the Appearances of Friendſhip: but he ſaid, he had early ſmelled out an ill de- deſign in all that matter; that he ſaw of what dangerous conſequence it was like to be; but yet, that he might fully diſcover what was at the bottom of it, he confeſſed , he ſeemed to aſſent to ſeveral things, which he deteſted : and that by this means he ſaw into their ſecret, and knew all the ſteps they made, he ſtill cau- tiouſly obſerving all that paſt among them till it ſhould be neceſſary for him to diſcover and cruſh this Cabal. I need not tell you how ſeverely this is cenſured, by thoſe who be- live it. I would rather hope, that it is not true, how poſitively ſoever it may be affir- med at *Rome*; but tho it is hard to reconcile ſuch a way of proceeding with the common rules of human Society and of Vertue, yet at *Rome* a *Zeal* for the *Faith* , and againſt *Hereſie*, ſuperſedes all the Bonds of *Morality* or *Hu- mainty* , which are only the common *Vertues* of *Heathens*.

In ſhort, what truth ſoever may be in this

par-

particular, relating to the *Cardinal*, it is certain that *Molinos* was clapt up by the *Inquisition* in *May* 1685. and so an end was put to all Discourses relating to him: and in this silence the business of the *Quietists* was laid to sleep, till the ninth of *February* 1687. that of a sudden it broke out again in a much more surprising manner.

The Count *Vespiniani* and his *Lady*, Don *Paulo Rocchi*, Confessor to the Prince *Borghese*, and some of his family, with several others, in all 70 *persons*, were clapt up. Among whom many were highly esteemed both for their *Learning* & *Piety*. The things laid to the charge of the *Churchmen* were their neglecting to say their *Breviary*; and for the rest, they were accused for their going to *Communion* without a going at every time first to *Confession*: and in a word, it was said, that they neglected all the exterior parts of their *Religion*, and gave themselves up wholly to Solitude and *inward Prayer*. The Countesse *Vespiniani* made a great noise of this matter; for she said, she had never revealed her *Method* of *Devotion* to any Mortal, but to her *Confessor*, and so it was not possible that it could come to their knowledge any other way, but by his betraying that *Secret*: and she said, it was time for people to give over going to *Confession*, if *Priests* made this use of it, to discover those who trusted their *secretest* Thoughts to them;

and

and therefore she said, that in all time coming, she would make her *Confeſſions* only to God. This had got vent, and I heard it generally talked up and down *Rome*: ſo the *Inquiſitors* thought it more fitting to diſmiſs *Her* and her *Huſband*, than to give any occaſion to leſſen the credit of *Confeſſion*; they were therefore let out of priſon, but they were bound to appear whenſoever they ſhould be called upon. I cannot expreſs to you, the Conſternation that appeared both in *Rome* and in many other parts of *Italy*, when in *a months* time about 200 *perſons* were put in the *Inquiſition*: and that all of the ſudden, a *Method* of *Devotion*, that had paſſed up and down *Italy* for the higheſt Elevation to which mortals could aſpire, was found to be *Heretical*, and that the chief promoters of it were ſhut up in *priſon*.

But the moſt ſurpriſing part of the whole ſtory, was, that the *Pope* himſelf came to be ſuſpected as a favourer of this new *Hereſy*: ſo that on the 13th. of *February* ſome were deputed by the *Court* of the *Inquiſition* to examin him, not in the quality of *Chriſts Vicar*, or *St. Peters ſucceſſor*, but in the ſingle quality of *Benedict Odeſcalchi*: what paſſed in that Audience, was too great a Secret for me to be able to penetrate into it: but upon this there were many and ſtrange Diſcourſes up and down *Rome*: & while we *Hereticks* were upon that asking, where was the *Popes Infallibility?*

I remember a very pretty *Anfwer* that was made me. They faid, the *Popes Infallibility* did not flow from any thing that was Perfonal in him, but from the care that Chrift had of his *Church*: for a *Pope*, faid one, may be a *Heretick* as he is a private man: but Chrift, who faid to *St. Peter*, *feed my sheep*, will certainly fo order matters that the *Pope* fhall never decree *Herefy*, and by confequence fhall never give the flock *Poyfon* inftead of the *Bread* of *Life*; while the *Popes Herefy* was only a perfonal thing, it could have no other effect but to damn himfelf: but if he decreed *Herefy*, this corrupted the whole *Church*: and fince Chrift had committed all the *flock* to the *Popes* care, it ought to be believed, that he would never fuffer them to pronounce *Herefy ex Cathedra*, as they call it. This had fome colour in it, that was plaufible: but the fhift of which another ferved himfelf, feemed Intolerable. He faid, the *Pope* could never decree *Herefy*: for which he argued thus: he muft be a *Heretick* before he can decree it; and upon that he gave me many Authorities to prove, that in the minute that the *Pope* became *a Heretick*, he fell *ipfo facto* from his Dignity; and therefore he faid, the *Pope* could not decree *Herefy*; for he muft have fallen from his *Chair*, and have forfeited his Authority, before he could poffibly do it: fo that he was no more *Pope*. This lookt fo like a Juggle of the *Schools*, that I confefs it

made

made no great Impreffion on me.   Imagine
what a thing it would be,to fee a *King* accufed
of *Treafon* by one of his own *Courts*; and then
you have fancied fomewhat that comes near
this attempt of the *Inquifition's* : which being
a *Court* authorifed by the *Pope*, yet had the
Boldnefs to examin himfelf: and it had certainly been an odd piece of News, if upon the
Popes Anfwers, the *Inquifition* had ftained him
with the Imputation of *Herefy*,and had lodged
him in the *Minerva*.   Upon the difcourfe to
which this gave occafion, I have heard the
Authority of the *Court* of *Inquifition* magnified
to fo Extravagant a degree, that fome have
afferted, it was in fome refpects *fuperiour*
even to the *Pope* himfelf.   Two days after
that, the *Inquifition* fent a Circular *Letter* to
Card. *Cibo*, as the chief *Minifter*, to be fent
by him all about *Italy*, of which I fend you a
Copy in *Italian* : for tho it ought to have been
writ in *Latin*, yet I do not know how it
came to be writ in *Italian* : for the writing it
in the Vulgar language, was cenfured not
only as an Indecent thing, but as that which
made the matter more publick; it was addreffed to all *Prelats*; and it warns them,
that wheras many *Schools* and *Fraternities*
were formed in feveral parts of *Italy*, in which
fome perfons, under a pretence of leading
people into the *Wayes of the Spirit*, and to the
prayer of *quietnefs*, they inftilled in them many

abominable *Herefies*; therefore a ftricte charge was given to diffolve all thefe *Societies* : and to oblige all the *Spiritual Guides* to tread in the known Paths : and in particular, to take care, that none of that fort fhould be fuffered to have the Direction of the *Nunneries*, Order was likewife given to proceed in the way of Juftice againft thofe who fhould be found guilty of thefe abominable *Errors.* After this a ftrict enquiry was made into all the *Nunneries* of Rome; for moft of their *Directors* and *Confeffours* were found to be engaged into this new *Method.* It was found that the *Carmelites*, the *Nuns* of the *Conception*, of the *Paleftrina*, and *Albano*, were wholly given up to *Prayer* and *Contemplation*, and that inftead of their *Beads*, and their *Hours*, and the other Devotions to *Saints*, or *Images*, they were much alone, and oft in the Exercife of *Mental Prayer*: and when they were asked, why they had laid afide the ufe of their *Beads*, and their antient *Forms*; their Anfwer was, that their *Directors* had advifed them, to wean themfelves from thefe things, as being but Rude Beginnings, and Hindrances to their further progrefs: they juftified alfo their Practice from thofe *Books* that had been lately publifhed by the approbation of the *Inquifitors* themfelves, fuch as *Molinos* and *Petrucci's* Books.   When report was made of this matter to the *Inquifition*, they fent Orders to take

out

out of the *Nuns* hands all thofe *Boaks*, and fuch Forms of *Devotion* as were written in that ftrain; and they required them to return again to the ufe of their *Beads*, and their other abandoned *Forms*, which was no fmall mortification to them.   The Circular *Letter* produced no great effects; for moft of the *Italian Bishops* were either extream unconcerned in all thofe matters, or wereInclined to *Molinos*'s *Method*: and whereas it was Intended, that this as well as all the other *Orders* that come from the *Inquifition*, fhould he kept fecret, yet it got abroad, and *Copies* of it were in all peoples hands, fo that this gave the *Romans* the more occafion to difcourfe of thefe matters, which troubled the *Inquifitors* extreamly, who love not to have the World look into their Proceedings, nor to defcant upon them: they blamed Card. *Cibo*, as if this matter was grown fo publick by his means: but he on the other hand blamed the *Inquifitors* for it, and his *Secretary* blamed both. It was alfo faid, that the *Pope* was not pleafed with Card. *Cibo's* conduct, and that he thought he had fuffered this matter to go too far, without giving a check to the *Inquifitors*, when it might have been more eafily done; wheras now matters are gone to that height, that many think they cannot end without fome very great Scandal. For the *Quality* of the *Prifoners* is confiderable;

fome

fome of Cardinal *Petrucci's Domefticks*, and both his *Secretary* and his *Nephew* were of the Number; and tho the *Cardinal* himfelf came to *Rome* foon after, yet he was there for fome time *Incognito*. It is generally belie-ved, that both he and the Cardinal *Caraffa*, and Cardinal *Ciceri*, who is Bifhop of *Como*, are in great apprehenfions of a ftorm from the *Inquifition*: and the Ceremony of giving them their *Hats* being fo long delayed, was generally afcribed to fome complaints that it feems the *Inquifitors* made; yet in Conclu-fion they appeared in *Publick*, and had there *Hats* given them. The Duke of *Ceri*, *Don Livio*, that is the *Popes Nephew*, is believed to be deeply engaged in the matter: for the Count *Vefpiniani*, who was firft feifed on, is his particular Friend and Favorite: and is a fort of a Domeftick of his. *Don Livio* him-felf is likewife a perfon of a Melancholy Temper, that is much retired; and this at prefent is enough to make a man pafs there for a *Quietift*. He went from *Rome* to a Houfe he has not far from *Civitavecchia*, to avoid, as was thought, the falling into the hands of the *Inquifitors*. The *Pope* writ oft for him, before he could prevail with him to return; and it was faid, that he did not think himfelf fecure even after all the Affu-rances that the *Pope* gave him, that no harm fhould come to him; for it might be juftly

enough

enough apprehended , that the *Inquiſitors,* who had been ſo hardy as to examin the *Pope,* would make no Ceremony with his *Nephew ,* if they found matter againſt him.

But among all that were clapt up; Father *Appiani* was the man that ſurpriſed the *Romans* the moſt: he was ſeiſed on the firſt Sunday of *April ;* he was eſteemed the learnedeſt and Eminenteſt *Jeſuite* that was in the whole *Roman Colledge.* This did not a little mortifie the *Society ;* one of their *Fathers* had approved of *Molinos's* Book , and now another was found to be engaged in this matter : upon which a *Prieſt ,* that was indeed no Friend to their Order , ſaid to me , *that this was their true Genius, to have men among them of all ſides ;* that ſo which ſide ſoever prevailed , they might have ſome among them , that ſhould have a conſiderable ſhare in the Honour of the Victorious. And thus if *Molinos's* Method had been eſtabliſhed , then they would have gloried as much in *Eſparza* and *Appiani,* as they are now aſhamed of them. It is likely that they had not diſcovered *Appiani's* favouring the party , otherwiſe no doubt they had been before-hand with the *Inquiſition ,* and had ſhut him up as they did *Eſparza ;* and ſo have covered, themſelves from the reproach of having a man that favoured *Hereſy* among them. But the Confidence of that *Society* is an Original ; and ſince
I have

I have this occasion to mention them, I will here digress a little from the business of *Quietism*, to give you account of some of their Practices at *Rome*, with relation to *English Affairs*, with which I was made acquainted during my stay there.

There is a *Jesuit* belonging to the *English* House, F. *Cann*, well known in *England*, by some of his *Writings*, and in particular by one against the *Oath of Allegeance*, in which he pleads for the *Popes* Power of deposing *Princes*; it seems he was sorry to see that the Discourse which he had writ against the taking that *Oath*, had no better effect, and that the *Papists* generally took it: so he resolved to carry this matter further, therefore tho he had no other Character but that of a *Father* of the *Society*; he proposed at *Rome*, that a formal *Oath*, abjuring the *Oath of Allegeance*, should be taken by all who had taken the other; and that for all that should be received to be *Students* in that House, in all time coming, they should be bound by an *Oath* never to swear the *Oath of Allegeance*: since he said, a time might come, in which it should be necessary for their Interests, that they should be under no such tie to a *Heretical Prince*: But because it was not safe for them to enjoin any new *Oath*, without an order from the *Court* of the *Rota*, according to the Forms there, it was necessary to present

fent a *Memorial* for this: and that ought to come from the *Protector of the Nation concerned*: So he ought to have addreffed himfelf to Cardinal *Howard*; but the *Cardinal's* temper, and his principles, with relation to Civil Obedience, were fo well known, that F. *Cann* thought to carry the bufinefs without his having any fhare in it. Yet he found himfelf miftaken; for the *Iudges* of the *Rota* were furprifed at the Propofition, and gave notice of it to the *Pope*, who lookt upon it as a thing of very bad confequence: and askt Cardinal *Howard*, if it had been fet on by any direction from him; for it feems his Name was made ufe of, tho without his knowledg. The *Cardinal* was furprifed at it, and highly refented the Impudence of F. *Cann:* He fent a Complaint of it to the *General* of the *Society*, who, to give the *Cardinal* fome content, gave *Cann* a Reprimand, and fent him out of *Rome:* But the *Iefuites* carry a Grudge in their Hearts to the *Cardinal* for this, and other things: and this appeared very vifibly during the Earl of *Caftlemain's* Embaffay: for tho he lodged for fome time in the *Cardinal's Palace*, yet he gave himfelf up fo intirely to the Conduct of the *Jefuites*, that the *Cardinal* was quite fhut out of the Councils: and while Fa. *Morgan* came at all hours to the *Ambaffadour*, even in his night Gown and Shippers, which was thought

an

an unufual thing at *Rome*, where publick
perfons live in an exactnefs of Ceremony:
once the *Cardinal* was made to wait in the
Antichamber, while the *Father* was within
entertaining the *Ambaffadour* in this lafy
drefs, who coming out in it, the *Cardinal*
was fo provoked at this Indignity, that was
done him, and at the *Iefuites* Infolence, that
he threatned to fling him down ftairs, if he
ever prefumed to come within his Houfe a-
gain in that Habit : and indeed, a *Cardinal*
makes fo great a figure in *Rome*, that fuch an
ufage of him was thought a little Extraordinary, but the *Cardinal* is of fo mild a temper,
and the *Iefuites* are fo violent, as to be reckoned the *Horns of the Beaft*, that no wonder if a Sympathy of temper made the
Ambaffador fall in more naturally with them.

But I will now return to the *Quietifts*,
from whom, the particular regard that I hear
to the Order of the *Iefuites*, has diverted me
fo long. The *Prifons* of the *Holy Office* were
full, and the Terrour of this matter had
ftruck fo many, that no body could guefs
when or where it fhould ftop. It is faid, that
the *Inquifitours* have found in fome of their
Examinations, that they have to do with
men that are learneder than themfelves: and
that their Prifoners are fteady and refolute. It
is alfo faid, that their Friends abroad have expreffed a great concern for them, and for
the

the caufe of their Sufferings, and that many Letters have been writ to the *Inquifitors*, wifhing them to confider well what they do to their Prifoners; and affuring them, that they will maintain their Interefts: and that they are ready to feal them with their Blocd. It is certain, the *Pope* and Cardinal *Cibo* are much troubled, to fee that this matter is gone fo far, and is now fo much talked of. Cardinal *Petrucci* is ftill much in the *Popes* favour, and was fuffered not long ago to go vifit *Molinos*, with whom he had a long converfation all alone, but the fubject and the effects of it are not known: yet a fevere Sentence is expected againft *Molinos*. Thofe that fpeak the mildeft, think he will be a Prifoner for life: but a little time will fhew more than I can prefume to tell you. It is a terrible thing to have the whole body of the *Regulars* againft one, who according to the eftimate that is made at *Rome*, are about 500000. Perfons, and of that number it is faid the *Iefuites* make 40000. In the City of *Naples* alone it is believed the *Regulars* and other Ecclefiafticks amount to 25000. fo it is very likely, that when fuch Bodies, and *Molinos* are in the ballance, *Cajaphas*'s Refolution may once more take place: *It is expedient that one man fhould die, rather than that thofe Nations of Regulars fhould perifh*, or their Trade and Profits be lefsned. But to come to an end,

D   the

the *Inquifitors* have prepared the world for any
Judgments that they may pafs in this matter,
by ordering one of their number, to draw up
a Cenfure of 19. Articles, which he pretends
to have collected out of the *Writings* and
Doctrines of the *Quietifts*, and thus by repre-
fenting them fo odioufly, they have as much
as in them lies, prevented thofe Compaffions
which may perhaps be kindled by the fufferings of thofe whom they may condemn as
guilty of thofe cenfured Opinions. I have
now given you all the Informations that I
could pick up of this matter, with all poffible fincerity; for I have reprefented this bufinefs to you, juft as it was fet before my felf,
without making any Additions to it, or inter-
pofing my poor judgment in fuch a matter,
which I leave to you, and to fuch as you are.
I conclude, referring you for a further light
into this Affair to the Cenfure of the *Inquifi-*
tors, which I procured in *Italian*, for tho probably it is written Originally in *Latin*, yet I
could not get a Copy of the *Latin* Cenfure,
and fo was forced to content my felf with
this that follows. It appears by it, how low
the ftudy both of *Divinity* and of the *Scrip-*
tures is funk at *Rome*: fome few ftrictures
will be found on the Margin of the *English*
Tranflation of this *Cenfur*, which I have added, becaufe fome perhaps may defire to fee
this, who do not underftand *Italian*.

                                   The

THE
CIRCULAR LETTER,

That was fent about *Italy*, by the
Order of the *Inquifition.*

Em^{mo} e R^{mo} Sig^e mio Off^{mo}

ESfendo venuto à notitia di quefta Sacra Con-
gregatione, che in diverfi luoghi d'Italia fi vadi-
no poco à poco erigendo, e forfe anche fi fiano
erette certe Scuole ò Compagnie, Fratellanze, ò
Radunanze, ò con altro nomi, ò nelle Chiefe, ò
nelli Oratorii, ò in Cafe private à titolo di Confe-
renze Spirituali, ò fiano di fole Donne, ò di foli
Huomini, ò mifti, nelle quali alcuni direttori Spirituali inefperti della vera via dello Spirito calcata
da Santi, e forfe anche malitiofi fotto titolo d'inftra-
dare l'anime per l'Oratione, che chiamano la
la Quiete, ò di pura Fede interna, ó con altri nome, benche dal principio apparifca, che perfuadino
maffime d'ifquifita perfettione, ad ogni modo da
certi principii mal'intefi, e peggio pratticati vanno
infenfibilmente inftillando nella mente de femplici
diverfi graviffimi errori, che poi abortifcono anco
in aperte Erefie, & abominevoli laidezze con dif-
capito irreparabile di quelle anime, che per folo
zelo di ben fervire à Dio fi mettono in mano di fim-
plice Direttori, come pur troppo è noto effer fequi-
to in qualche luogho. Hannò perció quefti miei
Em. Signori Colleghi Generali Inquifitori ftimato

op:

opportuno di fignificare à V. E. con la prefente che
fi fà circolare à tutti gli Ordinarii d'Italia ; acciò fi
compiaccia d'invigilare fopra qualfivoglia nuove
adunanze fimili diverfe dalle già praticate & appro-
vate ne luoghi Cattolici , e trovandone de tali onni-
namente , le abolifca ; ne permetta in avenire che
in modo alcuno ne vengano inftituite , & infifta,
che i Direttori Spirituali caminino la ftrada battuta
della perfettione Chriftiana , fenza affettare fingo-
larità di vie di Spirito, con avvertire fopra tutto, che
neffuna perfona fofpetta di novità fimili s'ingerifca à
diriggere ne in voce, ne in fcritto le monache , acciò
che non entri ne' Monafterii quella pefte , che pur
troppo potrebbe contaminare la fpiritual intentione
di quefte Spofe del Signore. Il che tutto fi ri-
mette alla prudenza dell' E. V. con che però non
s'intenda con quelle provifionali, che ella farà per
fare preclufa la via di procedere, anche per via di
giuftitia : quando fi fcopriffero in qualche perfona
tali errori non efcufabili. In tanto fi và quì digeren-
do la materia, per poter à fuo tempo avvertire il
Chriftianefimo degli errori da evitarfi. E le Bacio,
15. Febrari , 1687.

THE
CIRCULAR LETTER,

Put in *English*

Moft Eminent, or *Moft Reverend Lord:*

THIS Holy *Congregation* , having received Advertifement, that there are fome

in

in divers places of *Italy*, that by little and little are erecting, or perhaps that have already erected, some *Schools*, *Companies*, *Fraternities*, or *Assemblies*, under some other Denomination, either in *Churches*, *Chappels*, or in private *Houses*, under the pretence of *Spiritual Conferences*; and these consisting either only of Women, or only of Men, or of both Sexes together, in which some *Spiritual Guides*, that are unacquainted with the true *way of the Spirit*, in which the Saints have trod, and that are perhaps men of ill designs, do under the pretence of leading Souls by the *Prayer of Quietness*, as they call it, or of *Pure Inward Faith*, or under any other name, in which tho in the beginning that they carry men, by Maxims that are of the highest perfection, yet at last they by certain principles, that are ill understood, and worse practised, do insensibly infuse into the minds of the simple, divers grievous *Errors*, that do break out into open *Heresy*; and to abominable Practices, to the irreparable prejudice of those Souls, who out of their single Zeal to serve God well, put themselves in the hands of such simple *Directors*, which is too notoriously known to have fallen out in some places. In consideration of all this, my most Eminent *Lords* and *Colleagues*, the *Inquisitors General*, have thought fit to signify this to you, by this Circular *Letter*, which is sent to all the *Or-*

dinaries

dinaries of *Italy,* that ſo you may be pleaſed, to watch over all ſuch new Aſſemblies, that are different from thoſe that are practiſed and approved in other *Catholick* places : and that where you find any ſuch, you aboliſh them entirely, and ſuffer them not to be any further advanced ; and that you take care that *Spiritual Directors* ſhall tread in the *beaten Paths of Chriſtian Perfection*, without affecting any Singularity in the *Wayes of the Spirit*: and that above all other things, you take care, that no perſon ſuſpected of theſe Novelties, be ſuffered to thruſt himſelf into the direction of *Nunneries*, either by Word or Writing: that ſo this Peſt may not enter within thoſe Houſes; which may too much corrupt the Spiritual Intention of thoſe *Spouſes* of *Chriſt.* All this is referred to your prudence : but with all this proviſional care, it is not to be underſtood as if hereby the proceedings in the way of Juſtice, were to be hindred, in caſe any perſons are found to hold inexcuſable Errors. In the mean while, care is taken ſo to digeſt this matter, that *Chriſtendom* may be in due time advertiſed of thoſe Errors that are to be avoided.

Rome the 15. *of February,* 1687.

THE

THE
CENSURE
OF THE
Opinions of the *Quietifts,*
Prepared for the *Inquifition.*

Errori principali di quelli, che efercitano l'Oratione di Quiete, *co' le Rifpofte.*

LA Contemplatione, o vero Oratione di Quiete confifte in conftituirfi alla prefenza di Dio,
on un atto di Fede ofcura, pura, & amorofa, e di-
)oi fenza paffar più avanti, e fenza ammettere dif-
orfo, fpecie, ò penfiero alcuno, ftarfene cofi otio-
); par effer contrario alla riverenza dovuta à Dio il
eplicare quel puriffimo atto, il quale però è di tanto
nerito, e vigore, che contiene in fe, anzi fupera
on gran vantaggio tutti infieme li meriti delle altre
irtù, e perfevera tutt' il tempo della vita, mentre
on fi ritratti con un atto contrario: Onde non è
eceffario reiterarlo, e replicarlo.

CENSURA e RISPOSTA.

Niun' atto di Fede ci conftituiffe prefenti à Dio,
quale è dentro à noi per indifpenfabile neceffità
ella fua Immenfità, e però fpeffo dicevano Elia,
Michea, & altri Profeti: *Vivit Deus in cujus confpeĉlu*

D 4   *fto.*

fto. E con Agoftino dicono i Teologi : *In De*
vimus, movemur, & fumus. Dunque l'atto di Fede,
che fuppone l'eflere della Creatura, fuppone q
già prima nella prefenza di Dio, e folamente
raffegnatione di Spirito nelle braccie della Divi
Intorno à quefta all'hora fará contemplatione,q
do l'Anima contemplarà, e non farà otiofa, do
il primo atto di Fede ofcura, pura, & amorofa.
poi talfità evidente il dire, che non fono nece
altri buoni atti. L'Atto buono, per effer finit
migliorabile, per mezzo della continuatione di f
atti. Ne' la moltiplicatione di atti virtuofi e'
trario alla riverenza dovuta à Dio, perche I
non fi tedia, ò impedifce, effendo libero da'
paffione, & in tanto non conviene replicare
rivercntiali a' Maggiori del Mondo, in quanto
quefti, fecondo che porta l'efperienza,fono alter
impedibili, ó tediabili della vifta di fimili atti
quentati. L'atto dunque in fe fteffo buono, m
plicato fará un buono maggiore, e però da' Di
provato, a più rimunerabile, che un' atto
Nella Contemplatione poi fi ftà in atto di opera
non oftinatamente fopra l'attopaffato, effen
Contemplare l'operare mentalmente,ancorche
anco vi fi richieda.

II. Senza la Contemplatione, per mezzo
meditatione non può darfi un paffo nella Pe
tione.

Per meditarfi dal Chriftiano precifamen
Paffione di Chrifto, fi riflette, che per amor
Huomo tanto pati un Dio, unde può rifolvarfi
marlo, e volerlo obedire in che commanda, e
tere in prattica (con la gratia di Dio, che fempr
Noi) tal fanta deliberatione. Dunque permezzo
Meditatione può bene incaminarfi l'Anima alla
fettione. Anni fenza contemplare, e fenza med

pu

purche s'opri fecondo li Leggi, con l'ajuto di Dio
fi puo ogn' uno falvare ; non fi falva poi chi non è
perfetto, & Amico di Dio. Dunque è falfiffima
l'opinione contenuta nel fecondo Capo.

III. La Scienza, e Dottrina anche Teologica, e
Sacra, è d'impedimento, e repugnanza alla Contemplatione, della quale non poffono dar giuditio
gli Huomini Dotti, mà folo li Meditativi, e Contemplativi.

R. La Dottrina Teologica notifica ftabili in noi
l'Oggetto della Contemplatione, che dicono i
Quietifti effer la Divina Effenza. Dunque in noi
è compinibile con la Contemplatione, alla quale
fe la Teologia repugnaffe l'ifteffo farebbe effer
Contemplativo, e nulla faper d'Iddio Teolgal-
mente, e cofi Agoftino, e gli altri Santi Dottori,
e Luminari della Chiefa, perche erano fcientifici,
fi doverebbero incapaci effer ftati della Contemplatione. Il che è falfo, imperoche Dio, che in-
ftitui il Sacerdotio, come Miniftero il più degno,
non v'è ragione, che habbia voluto i Sacerdoti,
ma' che non foffero Contemplativi, già che volfe
col Sacerdotio unita la Scienza, mentre nella Sacra Scrittura minaccio per Ofea Profetta à chi di-
fprezzatore della Scienza efercitava il Sacerdotio.
*Tu repulifti fcientiam, & ego repellam te, ne Sacerdotio
fungaris mihi.* E tralafcio altre Scritture, e raggioni,
perche mi viene incaricata la breuità. In quanto
poi al che fi dice in quefto 3. cap. che della Contemplatione non poffono dar giuditio li Dotti, fi
vede apertamente, che l'ignoranza di quefti fpi-
ritelli fenza intelligenza hà una temerità di non
volar foggiacere all' emenda, per mezzo dell' Infal-
libile fentimento de' Scientifici.

IV. Non può darfi perfetta Contemplatione, fe
non circa la fola Divinità. I Mifteri dell' Incarna-
D 5   natione

natione, Vita, e Paffione del noftro Salvatore non fono oggetto di Contemplatione, anzi l'impedif-cono, onde devono dà Contemplativi tenerfi lontani; ò folo confiderarfi fpregiatamente.

℞. Se la Contemplatione è un affettione dell' Intelletto, e della Volontà con l'Ogetto, mediante la gratia di Dio, in un raccoglimento di Spirito, potrà la vita di Chrifto contemplarfi, perche à quella il Chriftiano può farfi prefente in Spirito, & affettive con atto di Fede, & Amore. Aggiongo che fe Chrifto venne à piantar Paradifi in terra per commiffione dell' Eterno Padre, come diffe il Profeta Ifaia, *Pofui verbum meum in ore tuo, ut plantos Cœlos, & fundes terram.* Dove la Parafrafe Caldea cofi legge: *Ut plantes Cœlos in terra*: Come dire (fi come l'intefe Girolamo) che piantaffe le contentezze negli Huomini difgratiati per il peccato originale : E fe i Contemplationi fi portano fopra fe fteffi alla Confolationi Divine nella loro Contemplativi, perche fi deve difprezzare, e tener lontano Chrifto, che è l'immediato Datore? Chrifto non impedifce l'atto del Contemplatione fe venne à compartirci perfettioni, e contenti fpirituali, che fono il fine de' Contemplativi.

V. Le Penitenze corporali, l'aufterità della vita non convengono alli Contemplativi, anzi meglio fi comincia la converfione dalla vita contemplativa, che dalla Purgativa, e dalle Penitenze. Ancora gli effetti della Divotione fenfibile, la tenerezza del Cuore, le Lagrime, e Confolationi fpirituali fi devono fuggire, anzi difpreggiare da' Contemplativi, come cofe repugnanti alla Contemplatione.

R. Le Mortificationi difpongono lo Spirito, acciò viva fopra le motioni del fenfo, e perciò tutti i fanti cominciarono à viaggiare verfo la Perfettione

con

con difcipline, Digiuni, &c. Dunque fe i Contemplativi hanno per fine anco la perfettione, ben li convengono le Penitenze, perche più fpedito fi renda alla Contemplatione, chi più tiene domate le alterationi del fenfo. E fe Dio promette nelle Scritture pardonar al Peccatore piante, che faranno dà lui le colpe, mà in neflun luogo del vecchio, ò nuovo Teftamento, per efferfi pofto nella Contemplatione. Dunque meglio fi comincia la converfione dalla vita purgativa, e dalle Penitenze, che dalla contemplatione.

VI. La vera Contemplatione deve fermarfi nella pura Effenza d'Iddio, fpogliata delle Perfone, e degli Attributi, e l'Atto di Fede di Dio cofi concepito, è più perfetto, e meritorio di quello, che riguarda Dio con le Perfone, & Attributi.

R. Le Perfone Divine, e gli adorabili Attributi di Dio hanno la raggione formale d'effer Oggetti di Fede, e d'Amore nel racoglimento delle noftre potenze, e nella raffegnatione dello Spirito, perche fono verità rivelate, e come Predicati Divini fuoni buoni in fe fteffi, & alle Creature. Donde può darfene vera contemplatione. Che poi l'atto di Fede di Dio fenza le Perfone, & Attributi concepito fia più perfetto, e meritorio di quello, che riguarda Dio con le Perfone, & attributi è falfità. Perche fe già il credere che Dio fia Trino, e fia giufto è atto di fede perfetto, e meritorio, e credere Dio vero nell' Effenza anco è atto meritorio e perfetto, farà l'atto con cui fi crede Dio vero erino, e giufto, più perfetto, e meritorio d'un altro atto, con cui folamente fi crede uno nell' Effenza, perche fi merita più per due atti dell' ifteffa virtù, che per un folo di quefti. (Havendoci Dio communicate le virtù fupranaturali non per far un atto folo virtuofo, mà per avanzarfi col' efercitio

citio di tali doni) Un' atto di fede, che equivale à due è più meritorio, e perfetto di un solo atto delli due: onde ben fi conclude contra la prima propofitione di quefto 6. Cap. che la vera, e perfetta contemplatione per eflere megliore deve fermarfi nella pura Eflenza di Dio, mà quefta nella Perfone, e negli Attributi.

VII. Nella Contemplatione s'unifce l'Anima immediatamente con Dio, onde non vi fi richiede Fantafmi, ò Imagini, ò fpecie di forte alcuna.

R. Nella Contemplatione ancorche in un certo modo s'unifca l'Anima immediatamente con Dio, cio è effettive, perche vi concorre l'intelletto a mirar Dio femplicemente, però fi richiede qualche fpecie per follicitare l'intellettuale habilità naturale à portarfi nella confideratione di Dio, fervendo la fpecie per oggetto mottivo all'Intelletto.

VIII. Tutti i Contemplativi nell' atto della Contemplatione patifcono pene, & angofcie fi gravi, che pareggiano, anzi fuperano, li tormenti dell' ifteffi Martiri.

R. Se (come dicono i Quietifti nel primo capo) la Contemplatione confifte nel farfi prefente à Dio con un atto di Fede amorofa, e poi ftarfene in otio, non è formalmente eflere tormentato, e patire pene più delli Martiri. E quantunque ad alcuno fpeffo fucceda nella Contemplatione angofcie, e dolori, ciò proviene da' altra caufa ò dal Demonio, permettendolo Dio, ò da' fiachezza di natura, che confuma il Corpo, ò da' motivi di Malenconia, ò da' foverchio fangue, che formontato alla tefta caggiona dolore. Mà moltiffimi àltri fi fono vifti nell' atto della Contemplatione, circondati di luce con fronte ferena, e bocca ridente, come Francefco di Paola fù offervato dà Luiggi XI. Rè di Francia, e finita la Contemplatione

tione reſtar tutti inondati di allegrezza, perche in quella vennero à viſta (ſemplicemente ben ſi) li ſpoſi, per reſtar concertato il Matrimonio frà Dio e l'Anima.

IX. Nel Sagrificio della Meſſa, e nelle Feſte de' Santi, è meglio applicarſi all'atto di pura fede, e Contemplatione, che alli Miſteri di eſſo Sacrificio, ò à conſiderare le attioni, e le coſe aptenenti alli medeſimi Santi.

R. Vive ingannato chi giudica entrare nella Contemplatione ſenza buona diſpoſitione dell'Anima; e perche la conſideratione delli Miſteri della Meſſa, e dell'eſempio de' Santi è preparamento ſpirituale, ancorche remoto, perciò ſtimarſi deve meglio, prima applicarſi il Chriſtiano alla conſideratione de i Miſteri della Meſſa, e delle attioni de' Santi, e poicia darſi alla Contemplatione con più Adobbo nell'Anima.

X. La Lettione ſpirituale de' libri, le Prediche, l'Orationi vocali, l'Invocationi de' Santi, e coſe ſimili, ſono d'impedimento alla Contemplatione, overo Oratione di Quiete, alla quale non ſi deve premettere preparatione alcuna.

R. Se in ogni profeſſione, e' maggiormente in quella della vera, e non fintionata ſpiritualità: *Nemo repente fit ſummus*, come l'eſperienza dimoſtra, perche è ordine della noſtra fiacca natura, co' cui ſi và accommodando la gratia per il noſtro camino all'ultimo termine dell'Eternjtà, che à *facilioribus fit incipiendum*; che perciò è grand' ignoranza, e preſontione entrare nell'Oratione di Quiete, prima d'altri eſercitii, e ſenza preparatione. Chi coſi entra, uſcirà ancora ſenz' alcun profitto.

XI. Il Sacramento della Penitenza, avanti la Communione non è per l'Anime interiori, e contemplative, mà per l'eſteriori, e meditative.

R. I

R. I contemplativi hanno folamente un' Anima che è può meditare, e può contemplare, & anco può ftar in peccato. Dunque il Sacramento della Penitenza prima della S. Communione, è neceffa-rio all' Anime contemplative.

XII. La Meditatione non riguarda Dio col lu-me della Fede, mà con il lume naturale in Spirito e verità, e però non hà merito appreffo Dio.

R. Se la meditatione non foffe meritoria appref-fo Dio, (*faltem aliqualiter de congruo.*) no' farebbe cofi famigliare alle Religioni, dove furono, e fono grand' Huomini fanali della S. C. R. ne fa-rebbe incaricata da' SS. Patriarchi, e da' Sommi Pontefici rimunerata con Indulgenze plenarie, co-me efercitio fpirituale, proportionato alli Amici di Dio, & à quelli, che abandonano le fallacie del mondo. Di Dio, come fi può conofcere l'efiftenza col lume naturale, e con la fede fopranaturale, cofi può darfi Meditatione che lo riguardi naturalmen-te, e Meditatione che lo riguardi con fede pura, e fopranaturale.

XIII. L'Imagini non folo interne, e mentali, mà anco l'efterne folite venerarfi da' fedeli, come fono quelle di Chrifto, e de' fuoi Santi, fono dan-nofe a' Contemplativi, onde devono fuggirfi, e to-glier via, acciò non impedifcano la Contempla-tione.

R. Quanto decretò, e decretarà la S. Madre Chiefa, à cui prefiede Direttore lo Spirito Santo tutto giovevole all' Vaffallaggio di Chrifto; però fe a' Fedeli la Chiefa ordina l'adorationi delle SS. Im-magini, non devono quefte ffuggirfi, ò toglier via, come nocive alla Contemplatione: nulladi-meno alcuni fguardi alla sfuggita verfo dette Im-magini non fono valevoli à far perdere la Contemp-platione, overo Oratione di Quiete al Contemplativo,

plativò, quale fe in ogni cafo la perde, proviene dalla fua troppa imbecillità, e per altro poi e più ampia l'Anima raggionevole; e maggine la gratia, che l'affifte di quello che fuppone quefte 13. Cap. Anzi la moderata confideratione di dette Imagini ferve à formar nell' Anima l'interno racoglimento, perche il contemplativo fi faccia regolare dalla Gratia.

XIV. Chi una volta fi è applicato alla Contemplatione non deve piu ritornare alla Meditatione, perche farebbe un paffare dal meglio al peggio.

R. E vero che è cofa mala paffare dal meglio al peggio, mà fpeffo conviene non poffedendo attualmente it meglio incaminarfi à poffeder il buono. E vero ancora, che effendo pontualmente nella Contemplatione, non fi deve lacciar quefta à fine di mettarfi nella Meditatione. Ancorche la Contemplatione fia migliore, non ritrovandofi il Chriftiano attualmente nella Contemplatione, non opera inconvenientemente applicandofi à meditare, perche conviene, che per ogni via, che Dio fi può mirare dall' Anima, fia da quefta riverentemente effequiata.

XV. Se nel tempo della Contemplatione vengono penfieri brutti, & ofceni, non fi deve ufar diligenza alcuna in fcacicarli, no' riccorrer ad alcu uno buon penfiero, mà compiacerfi di effere da' quelli moleftato.

R. Per non perderfi l'unione effettiva con Dio, che nella formale contemplatione fi trova, è atto di prudenza togliet via l'occafione, come è atto di fcioperaggine il trattenerfi con compiacenza, perche come dice S. Tomafo d'Aquino, *qui vult caufam, ex qua neceffariò, vel regulariter fequitur affectus, vult virtualiter effectum*, E lo Spirito Santo. *Qui amat periculum*

culum peribit in illo. Dunque fentendo in noi la rebellione del fenfo nella Contemplatione, ancorche fidati in noi fteffi, dobbiamo ufar ogni diligenza per fuperarla. Dovemo però raccommandarci alla Divinità, e chieder la fua gratia, per tranquillare i mali penfieri, diffondere le fue gioie nell' Anima, incalmare i fenfi alterati, *& ut fint afpera in vias planas.*

XVI. Niùn' atto ò affetto noftro interno, benche formato per mezzo della fede, e puro, ne piace à' Dio, perche nafce dall' Amor proprio, mentre non vi fia infufo dallo Spirito Santo, fenfa noftra induftria, e diligenza alcuna, onde quelli, che ftanno nella Contemplatione ò in Oratione d'affetti, devono ftare otiofi, ò afpettando l'influffo dello Spirito Santo.

R. A Dio folamente piacciono i' fuoi Doni, mà tutte quelle noftre Operationi, che da' Noi fi fanno con la fua Santa Gratia. Quindi tanto pier, profetta farà' la Contemplatione, quanto meno farà otiofa, purche il Contemplatore non fi lafci da' qualche fenfibile trafportare, preche perderia la Contemplatione, e gli fuccederabbe come alla Moglie di Loth, che per mirar indietro perfe il Camino. E poi temerità afpettare in otiofità l'influffo miracofa' dallo Spirito Santo, perche a' quei, che fono nell'Oratione di Quiete non fi deve il camino paffivo, mentre non hanno condegnità fopra i doni della Spirito Santo. Benfi fuccede alle volte che lo Spirito penetri l'Anima di chi ftà nell' Oratione d'affetti, mà per gratia particolare. Aggiongo contro la prima propofitione di quefto 16.capo. Li Quietifti dicono nel 12.capo che la Meditatione non hà merito appreffo Dio, perche non lo riguarda col lume della fede, dunque l'atto formato per mezzo della fede hà merito appreffo Dio, dunque è puro, e gli piace.   XVII.

XVII. Quelli che ſtanno nell' atto della Contemplatione, ò dell' Oratione di Quiete, ò ſiano Per-
ſone Religioſe, ò figli di famiglia, ò altri, che vi-
vono ſotto l'altrui commando, non devono in quel
tempo obedire & eſeguire gli ordini della Regola,
ò de' ſuperiori, per non interrompere la Contemplatione.

R. La contemplatione ancorche ſia in noi di gran
perfettione, perche non ci viene commandata da'
Dio, interrompendoſi non ſi pecca, mà eſſendoci
commandata da' Dio l'Obedienza a' Genitori, & à
ſuperiori, ſi deve obedire a' queſti, anco con laſ-
ciare l'attual Contemplatione, perche in riguardo
dell' ordine divino l'obedienza è preferibile nella
prattica, ancorche la Contemplatione ſia mol-
to più conſiderabile nella ſua perfettione objettiva.

XVIII. Devono i Contemplativi eſſer total-
mente ſpogliati dell' affetto di tutte le Coſe, che ri-
gettino a' ſe, e diſpreggino li Doni, e favori di
Dio, e ſi diſaffettionino dell' iſteſſa virtù, ò per
maggiormente ſpogliarſi d'ogni coſa, e viver meglio
a' ſe mediſimi, fare ancora quello, che ripugno
alla modeſtia, & all' Honeſtà, purche non
ſia eſpreſſamente contro li precetti del Decalogo.

R. Iddio favoriſce i Contemplativi con la Com-
municatione de' ſuoi boni, non per eſſere queſti
diſprezzati, mà per abbellirgli l'Anima, e fortifi-
cargli l'habilità naturale all' eſercitio della virtù.
Dvnque ancorche i Contemplativi non ſe ne debba-
no inſuperbire, devono ſopramodo ſtimarli, ò ſer-
virſene con humiltà di ſpirito: E ſe Dio vuole l'honeſtà come buona, ſono in obligo anche i Contemplativi eſſer honeſti, perche Iddio non hà fatto de-
creto, che privilegiaſſe i Contemplativi à non eſſer
ogetti alla raggione, ſu là quale ſi fonde la Modeſtia, e l'honeſtà della Vita.

E   XIX.

XIX. Li Contemplativi fono fogetti alle Violenze , per le quali reſtano privi dell' uſo del libero ar-
bitrio , ſi che ſe anco bene graviſſimamente pecca-
no eſteriormente , nondimeno interiormente non
fanno peccato alcuno ; onde ne anco devono Con-
feſſarſi di ció , che hanno fatto. Ciò ſi prova con l'e-
ſempio di Giob , il quale con tutto che non ſolo
ingiuriaſſe il Proſſimo , mà anco beſtemmiaſſe em-
piamente Dio , in ogni modo non peccava , perche
tutto queſto faceva per violenza del Demonio. E
per dar giuditio di queſte violenze , non ſerve la
Teologia Scolaſtica, e morale , mà è neceſſario
Spirito ſopranaturale , il quale in pocchiſſimi ſi
trova, & in queſti s'hà dà giudicare non l'interno
dall' eſterno , mà l'eſterno dall'interno.

R. Che in queſto Cap. 19. non ſolamente *latet*
Anguis ſub herba , mà apertamente ſi vede , che
ſotto nome di Contemplativi ſpirituali , vogliono
i Quietiſti eſſere debacanti ſenſuali. L'eſempio,
che adducono di Giob ben dimoſtra che no' hanno
intelligenza della Scrittura. Mai Giob peccò eſteriormente nè contro il Proſſimo , nè contro Dio,
quando parlò nel cap. 19. nel 6. verſo , come ben
dimonſtra , anco per mezzo del ſenſo litterale Pineda tom. 11. ſopra Giob c. 35. nè peccò contro
il Proſſimo, come nell' iſteſſo può vederſi , ſempre
fondata ſù la Dottrina de' SS. Padri ; che delle
Scritture, e inſegnano il vero ſenſo. E per dirla in
poche parole con altre raggioni, la gratia con la
quale Iddio ſempre ci aſſiſte , unita con la noſtra
cooperatione può ſuperare ogni aſſalto nemico. E
Chriſto lo diſſe à tutti in perſona di S. Paolo : *Suffi-*
cit tibi gratia mea. Dunque il Contemplativo non è
violentabile de venghi neceſſitato al peccato eſte-
fiori, &c;

THE

PRINCIPAL ERRORS,

Of thofe who Practife,

The Prayer of Quietnefs,

Cenfured and Refuted.

I. ERROR.

COntemplation, or *the prayer of Inward quietnefs*, confifts in this, *that a man puts himfelf in the prefence of God, by forming an obfcure Act of Faith, full of Love, tho fimple, and ftops there, without going further: and without fuffering any Reafoning, the Images of any things, or any Object whatfoever to enter into his mind: and fo remains fixed and unmoveable, in his Act of Faith: it being a want in that Reverence that is due to God, to redouble this fimple act of his: which is a thing of fo much Merit, and of fo great force, that it comprehends within it felf, and far exceeds the merit of all other vertues ; joyned together: and it lafts the whole courfe of a mans*

E 2   *life;*

life, if it is not discontinued by some other Act, that is contrary to it ; therefore it is not ne-cessary to repeat or redouble it.

The Censure and Refutation.

It is not an Act of Faith that puts us in the Presence of God : for he is within us by a necessary effect of the Immensity of his nature : therefore *Elias, Micaiah,* and the other Prophets said , *Vivit Deus in cujus conspecto sto. The Lord lives in whose presence I stand:* and it is upon the same reason that the Divines have said after S. Austin, *In Deo vivi-mus movemur & sumus* ; In God we live , we move, and have our being: so that an Act of Faith , that presupposes that the Agent is in being, supposes likewise that it is in the presence of God; & is indeed nothing else but a Resignation that the Creature makes of it self to God. Therefore *Contemplation,* even during that first obscure Act of Faith , that is simple and full of love, is carried on by the Soul while she looks at God, and not at all while she continues

Another would have thought that S. Paul should have been cited for this , rather than S. Aust., since he had said this first , Acts. 17. v. 28. but Rome is not the place of the World where the N. Testament is most read ; and this putting of ones self in the presence of God, can only mean the considering ones self as before him.

in an unmoveable state. It is then an Evident Falsehood to say, that other good actions are
not

not at all necessary: any good act being of its nature finite, may become alwayes better, by being often reiterated, and the multiplying the Acts of vertue cannot be contrary to the Reverence that is due to God, who being exempt from all passion, can never be troubled or wearied with Importunities, as great men are apt to be, who as Experience teaches, are often changed, disturbed, and become uneasy, when the same things are too often repeated to them. But with relation to God, when an act is in it self good, the repeating it is a progress in good; which is approved of God, and becomes more meritorious in his sight. Therefore the Soul in Contemplating, continues her Acts, and does not stick obstinatly to one single Act, *Contemplation* being still an Operation of the Mind, tho other things are likewise necessary.

II. E R R O R.

One cannot make one step towards Perfection by meditation, that being to be obtained entirely by Contemplation.

R E F U T A T I O N.

A Christian by meditating seriously on the Passion of Christ, and reflecting on that Love that made a God suffer so much for Mankind, may upon that resolve to love him again, and to obey all his Commands: and he may by the grace of God which is ever present to us, put

E 3

those

those good purposes in Execution : so that the
Soul may well advance towards Perfection by
Meditation : It may be also done without Meditation : for every one that lives according
to the Laws of God , may work out his
own Salvation by the help of God.   Now
since no man can be saved but he that is Perfect,
and a Friend of God's, then this *Article* is most
certainly false.

III. ERROR.

*All Study and Learning, even in sacred
Matters and in Divinity , is a Hindrance to
Contemplation : of which learned men are not a-
ble to make a true judgment, that being only to
be expected from those that are given to Meditation and Contemplation.*

REFUTATION.

The Study of *Divinity* makes known to us
the Object of *Contempla-*
tion : which as the *Quietists*
say , is the *Divine Essence:*
therfore it consists well with
Contemplation : and if the
Study of Divinity were op-
posit to this, then the ignorance of it is necessary to
make a man Contempla-
tive: and thus since *S. Austin* and all the other
holy Doctors and Lights of the Church, were
men Learned in this study, they must be looked
on as men that were Incapable of rising up to
Con-

*This Article is
falsly represented :
for the* Quietists, *as
all other* Mysticks,
*only except to that
dry learning which
is not accompanied
with an inward sense
of Divine matters.*

Contemplation: which is falfe: becaufe God,
who has appointed the Priefthood as the highe ft
degree of fervice done him, cannot be fuppofed to have Intended that the Priefts fhould not
be Contemplative perfons ; and it is plain ,
that God will have his Priefts to be knowin g:
fince in the Scriptures he threatens by *Hofea*
the Prophet fuch as defpifed knowledg, and yet
were in the Priefthood. *Tu repulifti fcientiam*
& ego repellam te ne facerdotio fungaris. Thou
haft rejected knowledg , and therefore I have re-
jected thee from the Priefthood. I pafs over other
Arguments from fcripture and reafon, becaufe I am ordered to be fhort : and as for
what is faid in this *Article* , that the *Learned*
cannot Iudge of Contemplation , it fhewes
plainly, that the Ignorance of thofe fpiritua-
lifts carries them to this boldnefs , of not
being willing to fubmit to that Correction ,
which they might expect
from that Infallible mean of　*Here is a new tribu-*
the Judgment of the Lear-　*nal of Infallibiliry.*
ned.

IV. E R R O R.

There is no Contemplation that is perfect,
but that which regards God himfelf; the My-
fteries of the Incarnation, and of the Life and
Paffion of our Saviour, are not the Objects of
Contemplation : on the contrary , they hinder
it: fo that Contemplative perfons muft avoid

them at a great diftance , and think of them only with Contempt.

REFUTATION.

If Contemplation is an affection that is raifed in the underftanding or the Will by its proper object by the help of the Grace of God, and that confifts in an Inward Recollection of the mind, then the Life of Chrift is a proper Object for it , fince a Chriftian can prefent this to his thoughts , and raife upon it an Act of Faith and love. Befides, Chrift came by a Commiffion from his Eternal Father to plant Paradife here on earth, according to that of the Prophet Ifaias , *Pofui verbum meum in ore tuo ut plantes Cœlos & fundes terram;* I have put my word in thy mouth that thou may plant the Heavens and eftablifh the earth ; or as the Chaldee Paraphrafe hath it , *ut plantes Cœlos in terra,* that thou may plant the Heavens in the Earth ; as if he had faid (as *S. Jerome* underftood the words) that thou may plant true joy in thofe minds , that were debafed by Original fin ; and how can it be imagined, that Contemplative perfons can rife above themfelves in their Contemplations to taft of Divine Joy's , if they muft keep at fuch a diftance

If we judge of this new Infallibility by this way of proving that Iefus Chrift is the proper Object of Contemplation , we will not much admire it ; but if this Article *is true , it looks liker* Deifm.

ſtance from Jeſus Chriſt, who is the Immediat giver of them; and deſpiſe him? Chriſt
is ſo far from hindring of Contemplation,
that he came into the world to diſtribute all
thoſe Perfections and ſpiritual Joys to which
the Contemplative aſpire.

V. ERROR.

*Corporal Penitences and Auſterities do not
belong to Contemplative Perſons : on the Contrary, it is better to begin ones Converſion by a
ſtate of Contemplation, than by a State of Pur-
gation or of Pennance ; and Contemplative
Perſons ought to avoid and deſpiſe all the effects
of ſenſible Devotion, ſuch as Tenderneſs of Heart,
Tears, and Spiritual Conſolations, all which
are contrary to Contemplation.*

REFUTATION.

Mortifications diſpoſe the Spirit to riſe
above the motions of ſenſe; and therefore it
is that all the Saints have begun their courſe
towards Perfection with Faſting and Diſci-
pline. And therefore if theſe Contempla-
tives deſign Perfection , they muſt practice
Pennance: ſince nothing renders a man ſo fit
for Contemplation, as to riſe above all the
Diſorders of Senſe. God in the Sciptures pro-
miſes to forgive the mourning Sinner; but
this is not promiſed to the Contemplative
in any place either of the Old or New Teſtament.   Therefore it is better to begin ones

Converſion with purgative Exerciſes and
Pennances, than with Contemplation.
VI. ERROR.

*True Contemplation muſt keep it ſelf fixed only
to the eſſence of God, without re-*

If this Article
is true, it con-
firms the ſuf-
pition of
Deiſm.

*flecting either on his Perſons or
his Attributes. And an Act of
Faith thus conceived, is more-
perfect and meritorious than
that which conſiders God with*
the Divine Attributes, or with the Perſons of
the Trinity in it.

REFUTATION.

The Perſons of the Trinity, and the Attributes of God, are the proper Objects of
Faith and love, while we recollect all the
Powers of our Souls, and reſign our ſelves
to God: for as theſe are divine Truths, that
are revealed to us, ſo the Attributes of God
are both good in themſelves, and good to
us, ſo that they are proper to raiſe in us a
true Contemplation. It is alſo falſe, that an
Act of Faith, that has God for its Object,
without conſidering his Attributes, or the
Perſons of the Trinity, is more perfect than
that which regards God in conjunction with
them. For if to believe that God is one,
and that he is Juſt, is a perfect and a merito-

Here one ſees what a thing ſchool rious Act of Faith,
Divinity is, by this way of recko- and to believe that
ning: but the value of acts riſes God is true in his
from the Intention of the mind,
and not from the Extenſion of the object. Na-

Nature is alfo a perfect and meritorious Act; then the Act by which God is believed to be true, juft and Three in One, is a more perfect and a more meritorious Act, than that in which he was confidered only as one in Effence. Becaufe a man merits more by two Acts of the fame vertue than by a fingle one only: for God has communicated fupernatural helps to us, not only for doing one Act of vertue, but that we may make an advance in fuch Acts. Therefore one Act of Faith, that is equivalent to two others, is more meritorious and perfect than any one of thefe two. Therefore we may juftly conclude againft the firft branch of this *Article*, that true and perfect Contemplation raifed to its higheft pitch, muft not only regard God in his Effence, but likewife in his Perfons and Attributes.

VII. ERROR.

The Soul becomes immediatly united to God in Contemplation; fo that there is no need of Phantafms, Images, or any fort of Reprefentation.

REFUTATION.

Tho it is true, that the Soul in fome fort unites her felf immediately to God in Contemplation, that is, by a Union of Affections; for the Underftanding beholds God fimply, yet fome Ideas are

This is not meant of pure Ideas, but of grofs Phantafms.

ne-

neceffary for exciting the natural force of the Underftanding, and to carry it to look at God: which Idea is a fort of Object that moves the Underftanding.

VIII. ERROR.

All contemplative perfons fuffer in the Act of Contemplation fuch grievous Torments, they feem to furpafs even the fufferings of the Martyrs themfelves.

REFUTATION.

If Contemplation confifts (as the *Quietifts*

This Article is alfo falfly reprefented; for the Quietifts *only mean, that Souls fuffer many inward Agonies in a contemplative ftate, of which all the Books of the My-*fticks *are full; and which they call the great Defolation.*

pretend it does) in this, that the Soul puts her felf in the prefence of God, by an act of Faith, full of Love, and after that continues idle: this is not the being formally tormented, or the enduring more than the Martyrs fuffered: and tho it is true in fome fort, that Pains and Miferies come after Contemplation, this flows either from the Devil, to whom upon that occafion God gives leave to try thofe perfons, or from fome weaknefs in Nature, that oppreffes the Body, from Melancholy, or an abundance of Blood, that raifes Headaches, or from fome other unknown Caufe. But many others have appeared to be in the very Act of Contemplation, as it were environed with Light,

and

and have looked with a ferene, and fometimes with a fmiling countenance ; which *Lewis* the XI. of *France* obferved in *Francis a Paula*; and they have been as it were overflown with Joy, when the Contemplation was over ; having been admitted in it, to fee their Bridegroom in that fimple Act, in which there paffes as it were a Marriage between God and the Soul.

IX. ERROR.

During the Sacrifice of the Mafs, and on the Feſtivals of the Saints, it is better to apply ones felf to an Act of pure Faith, and to Contemplation, than to the Myſteries of that Sacrifice, or to confider the Lives of thoſe Saints.

REFUTATION.

He is much deceived, who thinks to arrive at Contemplation without a due difpofition of Soul for it : and therefore the confideration of the Myfteries of the Mafs, and of the Examples that the Saints have fet us, is a fpiritual preparation for it, tho it may be

The Quietifts *only mean by this, that if a man in an act of outward devotion is carried to Contemplate, he is not to hold his mind to the outward devotion.*

only a remote one : therefore a Chriftian ought to fet himfelf firft to confider the Myfteries of the Mafs, and the Lives of the Saints, and then apply himfelf to Contemplation, having prepared his Soul duly for it.

X. ERROR.

X ERROR.

The reading of Spiritual Books, Sermons, Vocal Prayer, the Invocation of Saints, and all such things, are hindrances to Contemplation, which is only attained by the Prayer of Q uietness, *to which it is not necessary to premise any preparation whatsoever.*

REFUTATION.

If in every profession, but chiefly in a true and unfainedly spiritual Temper, that Maxim holds good, *Nemo repente fit summas,* No man attains to the height all of the sudden, which daily experience demonstrates; then it is but suteable to the feebleness of our Nature, to which the Divine Grace accommodates it self, that in our Journey towards that heighth of Eternity, *à facilioribus fit incipiendum,* we must begin with those things that are easier; therefore it is great Ignorance or presumption to enter into the *Prayer of Quietness* before other exercises, and without due preparation. And he who begins his course thus, will end it without any fruit.

The Quietists *only mean, that no general Methods carry men to Contemplation, and that it is the effect of a special Grace.*

XI. ERROR.

The Sacrament of Pennance before Communion, is not for contemplative Souls, that live in this inward state; but only for those that are in the Exteriour and Meditative state.

RE

REFUTATION.

These Contemplative persons have but one Soul, which at some times meditates, and at other times contemplates: and that may *This of one Soul is ridiculous.* come to be in a state of sin. Therefore the Sacrament of Pennance is necessary even for those Contemplative Souls, before they go to Communion.

XII. ERROR.

Meditation does not look at God with the Light of Faith, but only in a natural Light, in Spirit and in Truth: and therefore it is not meritorious before God.

REFUTATION.

If Meditation were not in some sort at least in the way of Congruity, meritorious before God; it could not be so much practised in all Religious Orders, from whence there have come, and *The Quietists only condemn a dry and Mechanical Meditation.* daily there does come, so many of the shining-lights of the Holy *Roman Church*: nor would it have been set on so much by their Holy *Patriarchs*, nor rewarded by the *Popes* with Plenary Indulgences, as a spiritual Exercise suteable to the Friends of God; and to those who had abandoned the Snares of this present World. But as one may know the Existence of God by the Light of Nature, as well as by a supernatural Faith, so likewise some

Me-

Meditations look at God, only with the Light of Nature ; and others are Acts of a Supernatural Faith.

XIII. ERROR.

Not only inward and mental Images , but those outward ones which are worshipped by the Faithful, such as the Images of Christ and of his Saints, are hurtfull to contemplative Persons, and they ought to be avoided and removed, that so they may not hinder Contemplation.

REFUTATION.

All things are useful to the Service of Christ, that either is decreed, or that may be decreed by the Holy *Mother Church*: in all whose Consultations the Holy Ghost presides and directs them. Therefore if the Church appoints the *Adoration of Images*, none of the Faithful ought to avoid them,

Here, notwithstanding all our Representers in England, you see the Adoration of Images is so received at Rome, that it is a Crime to think that the most perfect may be above it.

or remove them as hurtful to Contemplation, and some secret looks towards these Images, is no way likely to make a man fall from the heighth of Contemplation; or the *Prayer of Quietness*; from which if he falls at any time, it flows from his own great Instability, since the reasonable Soul is a Nobler being, and the Grace that it receives, is of a higher nature,

ture, than is fuppofed in this Article.
Therefore a moderate regard to *Images* will
ferve to confirm the Soul in her inward Re-
colletion, if a Contemplative man regulates
this by the help of the Grace of God.

XIV. ERROR.

He that has once applyed himfelf to Contem-
plation, muft never return to Meditation ; for
this were to fall, from a better State to a
worfe.

REFUTATION.

It is true, that it is an ill thing to go from
better to worfe ; but it is oft
times good for a man, that
cannot attain to that which
is *better*, to content himfelf
with that which is *good.* It
is alfo true, that while a man
is in Contemplation, he ought not to let
that go that he may turn himfelf to Meditation. Yet tho Contemplation is ftill the better State, when a Chriftian is not actually in
Contemplation, it is not Inconvenient for
him to apply himfelf to Meditation: becaufe
the Soul ought to follow God with all due
Reverence, in all thofe ways in which he
may lead her.

This is only meant
by the Quietifts,
of returning to a
Mechanical way of
Meditation.

XV. ERROR.

If foul and impure Thoughts come into the
mind while one is in Contemplation, he ought to
take no care to drive them away: nor to turn

himfelf

himself to any good thoughts, but to have a complacence in the trouble that he suffers from them.

REFUTATION.

It is a piece of prudence in a man who being in Contemplation, would not lose that union by which he is united to God, to avoid every thing that may occasion it; as on the contrary, it is a strong piece of neglect to entertain that with complacence which must make one lose it, as St. *Thomas* of *Aquin* says, *He that loves the cause from which any effect follows, either naturally, or at least commonly, does vertually love the effect it self :* And the Holy Ghost says, *He that loves danger, shall perish in it.* Therefore a man who being in Contemplation, feels the Rebellion of the sensible part, he ought to use all diligence to overcome in whatsoever a state he may be in. He ought therefore to recommend it to God, and to implore his Grace to quiet all those evil thoughts: that so his joy being spread abroad in the Soul, all the disorderly motions of sense may be calmed, *& ut sint aspera in vias planas,* That what is rough may be made smooth.

This is only so to be understood, that according to the rules given by all the My-sticks, *when ill thoughts come into a mans mind, the best may to overcome them, is rather to neglect them, than to struggle much against them.*

XVI.

XVI. ERROR.

No inward Action or Affection, tho formed by the vertue of Faith, is pure or pleasing to God: because it rises out of self-love , unless it is infused in us by the Holy Ghost, without any Industry or Diligence used by us: therefore they that are in the state of Contemplation or of Prayer, or inward Affections, ought to continue in a state of suspence, waiting for the miraculous Influence of the H. Ghost.

REFUTATION.

God is not only pleased with all his own Gitts, that are in us, but with every thing that is done by us, with the help of his Grace: therefore our Contemplation will be so much the more perfect, the less inactive we our selves are: provided that the Contemplative person does not suffer himself to be carried away by any sensible Object ; for by that he would fall from that State, and become as *Lot's* Wife, who was stopt short, because she looked behind her. It is then a rashness to keep our selves in an unactive state, and in it to look for the miraculous Influence of the H. Ghost. For all that are in the *Prayer of Quietness,* must not expect to be led into this Passive State, since they have not a Condignity sute-

This is indeed down-right Enthusiasm , yet much of this strain will be found in all the Writings of the Mysticks.

able

able to thofe Gifts. Tho' fometimes the H. Ghoft does penetrate the Souls of thofe who are in this prayer of inward affection, but this is the effect of a particular Grace: I add againft the firft branch of this *Article* that the *Quietifts* fay in the 12*th Article*, that Meditation is ofno merit in the fight of God, becaufe it does not look at him with the Light of Faith ; from which I infer, that an Act formed by the Power of Faith, is meritorious before God , and by confe-quence , it is pure and acceptable to him.

XVII. ERROR.

Thofe who have arrived at the State of Contemplation , and the Prayer of inward Quietnefs, being Religious Perfons, or being under the Authority of Parents, or any other fuperiours, are not bound to obferve their Rules, or to obey their Superiours, while they are in Contemplation , left that Interrupt it.

REFUTATION.

Altho Contemplation is an Act of high Perfection , yet fince it is not *This the* Quietifts commanded by God , it may *deny, as an Imputa-* be interrupted without fin: *tion caft upon them.* and fince Obedience to Pa-rents and fuperiours, is commanded by God, that ought to take place , and even Contem-plation ought to be difcontinued in order to it. And therefore confidering the Order that God has fetled , that Obedience ought to be

pre

referred to Contemplation , tho the latter is
s to its objective Perfection much more va-
iable than the former.

XVIII. E r r o r.

Contemplative perfons ought to divest them-
felves of all affections to all
things: they ought to reject   All the *Mysticks,*
nd defpife all Gods gifts   and in particular
nd favours , and to strip   *Sr. Philip Nerius,*
hemfelves of all Inclinations   have often done
ven for vertue it felf; and in   things that fee-
rder to this totall abnega-   med ridiculous &
ion of all things , and that   abfurd , as the
hey may live better within   higheft excercifes
hemfelves , they ought even   of Mortification
                                     and Humility.
o do that which is contrary to Modesty and de-
ency; provided that it be not exprefly contrary
o fome of the ten Commandments.

R e f u t a t i o n.

When God favours Contemplative Perfons
fo far, as to communicate any of his blef-
fings to them , thefe things ought not to
be defpifed , but to be confidered as Favours that tend both to beautify the Soul,
and to fortify her in the exercife of Vertue : fo that tho Contemplative Perfons
ought not to be lifted up with them ,
yet they ought to value them highly , and
to make ufe of them with all Humility of
Spirit : and fince God confiders *Decency* as a
fort of Goodnefs , Contemplative perfons

ought

ought to be *decent* in all things: for God has not by any special Decree exempted them from the Rules of Reason, upon which all the *Modesty* and *decency* of Life is founded.

XIX. ERROR.

Contemplative Persons are subject to violent Commotions, by which they lose the exercise of the Freedom of their Will. So that tho they may fall into most grievous Sins, as to the exteriour Act, yet they do not at all sin inwardly: And so they are not bound to confess that which they have done. All this is proved by the example of Job, *who tho he not only said things that were very Injurious to his Neighbour, but had blasphemed God most Impiously yet he did not sin in all this: because all was done by the Violence of the Devill. In order to the judging of these Violences, neither the Learning of the Schoolmen or of the Casuists, is of any use but a supernatural Spirit is necessary, which is to be found in very few persons: now these are the only Competent Iudges, who must not judge of the Internal by the External; but on the contrary, of the External by the Internal.*

This the Quie-tists reject as a Calumny, to render them justly odious to all the world

R E.

REFUTATION.

In this Article the Snake does not hide himself in the Grafs, but shews himself very visibly : since by this it is plain, that the *Quietists* will be senfual *Libertines* under the name of Spiritual and Contemplative Perfons. The Example that they bring of *Job* shews clearly how little they underftand the Scripture. *Job* did not fin outwardly , neither

But it is very poorly refuted, certainly Job faid many very hard things, which God who knew the fincerity of his heart , and the ftrength of his temtations, did not lay to his charge.

againft his Neighbour nor againft Gcd in what he faid , cap. 19. ver. 6. as *Pineda (tom.2. in Job* 235) has evidently proved from the literal fenfe of the words : he did not fin againft his Neighbour, as appears by the Expofitions of the Holy *Fathers* , from whom we are to learn the true fenfe of the Scriptures. And to end this matter in a few words, that Grace with which God affifts us at all times, is fuch, that we co-operating with it , may overcome all the Temtations of our Enemies. And Chrift has faid to all in the perfon of *S. Paul*, *My Grace is fufficient for thee* : therefore a Contemplative Perfon cannot be pufhed on by any violence or neceffity whatfoever, to any External Act of Sin.

F 4   *It*

It is not eafie to judge whether thefe *Articles* are faithfully drawn out, or truly, reprefented: for it is probable, that *Malice* has a large fhare in fome of them, chiefly in this laft, which leads to down-right *Libertinage*; tho' others have rather fufpected, that all tended to an Elevated *Deifm*: yet it is certain, that if there is much Poifon in thefe *Articles*, the Antidote of the *Cenfure* is fo feeble, that it cannot have a ftrong Operation; and it fhews how little the *Scripture* and true *Divinity* is underftood at *Rome*.

POSTSCRIPT.

IN the former *Letter*, I told you all that I could learn of this matter, during my ftay at *Rome*, but having left it in *Iuly*, I prevailed with one to give me an account of the Conclufion of this Affair, of which I fend you a Copy: for tho I know all the *Gazettes* of *Europe* will be full of the Decifion and end that is believed to be put to the bufinefs of *Quietifm*, yet you know too well, how little one ought to depend on fuch Relations: all the newes of this matter, will either be that which is writ by the direction of the *Inquifition*, or by the Strangers that are there, and pick up fuch things as they find among the *Romans*, who are ever true to the old Cha-

Character that *Juvenal* gave of that *City*,
   Sequitur fortunam, ut femper, & odit
Damnator.

Therefore I will give you an account of
this bufinefs, on which you may depend, in the
words of a Letter writ me from *Rome*.

Now this great Affair, upon which men
have fo long lookt with fo much expectation,
is at an end: and a party that was believed to
be a Million ftrong, is now either quite extin-
guifht, or at leaft oppreffed with a great deal
of Infamy : and Mr. *Molinos*, who has lived
above twenty years in this *City*, in the higheft
Reputation poffible , is now as much hated
as ever he was admired: he is not only confidered as a Condemned , and an Abjured *Here-*
tick, but he is faid to have been convicted of
much Hypocrify, and of a very lewd courfe
of life; which is fo firmly believed by the
Romans, that he was treated by them on the
day of his Abjuration, with all poffible In-
dignities ; but the people as they fhewed their
affections to him, by their cries of *Fire*, *Fire*,
fo were ready to have facrificed him to their
rage, if he had not been well defended by the
Sbiri and Guards that were about him. And
it would be a crime enough at prefent, to recommend a man to the care of the *Inquifitors*,
if he fhould feem to doubt either of his Herefy, or of the Scandals of his life. All the
party is extreamly funk : Cardinal *Petrucci*
F 5   himfelf

himself lives in *Rome* as if he were in a defert;
for no Body goes to vifit him, and he ftirs as
little abroad: nor is it thought that he will
efcape: there are four fent by the *Inquifition*
to his Diocefs of *Jeffi* to examin his behaviour there : there is alfo a difcourfe, that has
lately appeared at *Rome*, that was fecretly printed, of which he is fufpected to be the Author,
which is an *Apology for Quietifm*, that gives
great offence. It is faid, that the *Inquifitors*
had full proofs againft *Molinos*, by fourteen
Witneffes; of whom eight indeed came and
offered their Depofitions of their own accord,
and the other fix were forced to declare the
truth, which raifes the Credit of their Tefti-
mony: fince his Abjuration, it is faid that many of his Followers have abjured in private,
and that befides the Prifoners that are in their
hands, great numbers come in every day to
accufe themfelves, and to offer themfelves to
pennance, thefe are all very gently difmiffed
by the *Inquifitors*, who are now as much cenfured by the *Romans* for their exceffive mild-
nefs, as ever they have been blamed by others
for their rigour: and thofe fecret Abjurations
are believed to be all the Severity that they
will practife on this Occafion; for it is faid that
even *F. Appiani* the *Jefuite* will be abjured in
fecret; tho fome fay, he is madd, others that
he is become deaf and dumb, and not a few
believe that he is dead: fo uncertain are all
Reports

Reports at prefent. In a word, the hatred of the prefent *Pontificate* appears very vifibly upon this Occafion: the *People* affecting to fhew a very extraordinary rage againft a perfon, and a party, that has been fo much favoured and fupported by the *Pope*: fo that this matter comes clearly home to him, and wounds his Reputation extreamly; all this raifes the credit of the *Jefuites*, who value themfelves upon the zeal and the conduct of their *Society* upon this Occafion. All the *Popes* Enemies, the *Jefuites*, the *French Party*, and the body of the *People*, that are Malecontented and weary of him, and his long and dull *Reign*, fhew the Pleafure they have in aggravating this matter againft him: they fay, this is the firft time that ever any *Herefy* made *Rome* its Seat, where it choofed to neftle it felf; but it is yet more ftrange, that it fhould have continued there above twenty years, notwithftanding all that multitude of *Spyes* that the *Inquifition* has every where; that the *Pope* fhould have fhut his Ears againft all Complaints, fo that this Doctrine had gained fo great Authority, that thofe who attackt it, paffed for *Hereticks*, or Calumniators at leaft, and that even after all the Difcoveries that have been made, that the *Pope* was known to favour *Molinos* fecretly, and was fo hardly brought at laft to confent to the Condemnation, in which it is faid, that nothing prevailed on him till
the

the *Cardinal's* informed him of the Scandals of *Molinos's* Life, that were proved: this was indeed a matter that could fall within the *Popes* underſtanding; for the points of Doctrine are believed to be above it. All theſe things concur to increaſe the Contempt under which the preſent *Pontificate* lies; yet as for thoſe Scandals of *Molinos's* life, I do not know what to believe : many will not believe them, and think they are only Impoſtures given out to render him odious; for if they had been true, and well proved, it is ſaid, that the *Cenſure* would have been ſeverer; for a perpetual *Impriſonment*, and the ſaying his *Credo*, and the fourth part of the *Roſary* every day, are mild Puniſhments, if he is found to have been ſo flagitious a man, and ſo vile a Hypocrite, as is given out. His own Behaviour at the *Minerva* did not look, either like a Man, that was much confounded with the Diſcoveries that had been made, or that was very Penitent for them, or for his *Hereſy*: ſo that the Mildneſs of the *Cenſure*, to a Man that ſhewed ſo little humility or repentance, ſeems to flow rather from the Defectiveneſs of the Proofs, than from the gentleneſs of the *Tribunal*. I confeſs, I was not a Witneſs to what paſſed in the *Minerva*; for as I would not venture in the Crowd, ſo both Money and Favour was neceſſary to accommodate a man well on that occaſion, where not only

a

a general Curiofity brought a vaft confluence of People together, to fee the iffue of a Bufinefs that has been fo long in fufpence, but a particular Devotion : for the *Pope* had granted a *General Indulgence* to all that fhould affift in that Solemnity : but I will give you the account as I had it from Eye-witneffes. *Molinos* was well dreffed, new trimm'd, in his Prieftly Habit, with a cheerful Countenance, that as was faid by his Enemies, had all the Charmes on it, that were neceffary to recommend him to the fair Sex. He was brought from *Prifon* in an open Coach, one *Dominican* being with him in it. He was at firft placed for fome time in one of the *Corridori of the Minerva* : he looked about him very freely, and returned all the Salutes that were made him : and all that he was heard fay, was, *That they faw a man that was defamed, but that was Penitent (Infamato ma Pentito.)* After that he was carried to dinner, where he was well treated, that being to be his laft good Dinner. After Dinner, he was brought into the *Church*, as in a Triumph, carried on the fhoulders of the *Sbiri* in an open Chair : when he was brought to his place, as he made his Reverence very devoutly to the *Cardinals*, fo there was no fhew of Fear or of Shame, in his whole Deportment. He was chained, and a Wax Light was put in his hand, while two ftrong-lung'd *Fryers* read his *Procefs* aloud, and

and care had been taken to lay matters so, that as some of the *Articles* were read, all should cry *Fire, Fire.* When he came back to *Prison,* he entred into his little Cell, with great Tranquillity, calling it his *Cabinet,* and took leave of his *Priest* in these words, *Adieu Father, we shall meet again at the Day of Judgment, and then it will appear on which side the Truth is, whether on my side, or on yours.* So he was shut up for *Life.* Yet after all I find none of the wise men here think that the thing is at an end; but that the Fire which seems to be now extinguished, will break out with more violence; for one of his *Followers* had the boldness to tell the *Inquisitors* to their face, that they were a Company of Unjust, Cruel, and Heretical men; and compared their Treatment with that which Christ had met with, and yet even he has escaped upon an Abjuration, as is pretended. The Reasons that are given for this extraordinary Gentleness of the *Inquisitors,* who are seldom accused for erring on this side, are both the Numbers of the *Party,* who might be much irritated by publick Examples, and also the great Credit that their *Doctrine* has from the *Mystical Divinity,* that is authorised by so many *Canonisations:* for it is said, that from several parts the *Inquisitors* have brought together above twenty thousand of *Molino's Letters* : whose Correspondence

was

was fo vaft, that fome give out, that the *Poft* of the *Letters*, that were brought him the day in which he was feifed on, rife to twenty Crowns. And I heard a *Divine* of *Rome* confefs, that they have fuch *Authorities* for moft of their *Tenets*, that they will never be beat out of them, by the force of their *School Divinity*, therefore he thought it was neceffary to condemn them by a formal Sentence, in which the Authority of the Church was to be interpofed. Moft of the condemned *Articles* are nothing but an Invidious Aggravating of the Doctrine of *Predeftination* and *Grace* Efficacious of it felf, and of Immediat Infpiration: for all the hard Confequences that are pretended to be drawn, either from the one or the other of thefe Opinions, are all turned into fo many *Articles*, and condemned as fo many Impious Doctrines; but you will be better able to judge of this matter when you fee all that the *Inquifitors* will think fit to print concerning it.

A

A SECOND
LETTER

Writ from

R O M E,

Containing some Particulars, relating
to the

INQUISITION.

SIR;

MY laſt to you, together with the *Advertiſement* which was ſent me from *Rome*, related wholly to the Affairs of the *Quietiſts*; but becauſe I know your Curioſity will perhaps go further, and that you expect ſuch *Obſervations* from me, as you fancy me capable to make, in a *Countrey* where I have now made ſo long a ſtay, that it is my own fault, if I have not been able to ſee a little further than Common

Tra-

Travellers do; therefore I will try what I can say that may please you.

I am, as you know, no Searcher into *Manuscripts*, or the Curiosities of *Libraries*, nor can I bring my self to so dry a study as is that of *Medals*, or *Inscriptions*. I had rather be beholding to the Labours of others, for the Discoveries they have made in those matters, than wear out my Eyes and spend my Time in the reading and Deciphering those *Remains* of Antiquity. I love all that knowledg, which, with how much difficulty soever it may be acquired, feeds the mind with some useful Ideas: but as for that knowledg which carrys one no further, then that such a *Word*, or such a *Hierogliphick* signified such a *thing*, and that gives the mind no matter to work on, and raises no game at which it may fly, it has not charm enough to work on so lasy a man as I am. I confess, my studies, and my way of Life would have carried me more naturally into matters of *Religion*, or into the *Politicks*: but as to the former, *Italy* is not a Country, where a man either can or dare reason upon these Subjects: for their ignorance is such, that no man can profit much by their conversation on those heads: besides that, it is not safe to do it. The *Italians* are too well bred, to attack a man on that Argument; and they know their own Ignorance so well, and have so high an Opi-

nion

nion of the *Learning* of the *Hereticks*, that they are sure never to provoke any of them : and he were a very bold and Indiscreet man, that would begin the dispute with them : so after all, *Newes* and *Politicks* is all that Remains and you know I am idle enough both to think and to talk of these upon occasion : yet I must confess, that I find so many of my *Reflections* in Dr. *Burnets Letters*, that I have got sent me from *Leghorn*, that if I had not seen these, I had very likely writ you a grea many of those that are already set out by him, with so much advantage, that I find the best part of all my *Observations* are already made by a better Pen : but I, who have as great an Aversion from copying, as he says he has will avoid the saying any one thing that I find in his *Letters* : and will only speak of those Places that he did not see, or of those matter which he had not time enough to enquire af ter, or to observe ; and since the former *Let ter*, contained such a long and serious recita of a matter, that if it fixed your attention, yet must have wearied it, I will now divert you a little, with some *Storys*, that will be more agreeable ; and then I will return to more se rious *Subjects*. I will begin with some relating to the *Inquisition*. I told you in my former *Letter*, of a great many *Prisoners* in the *In-quisition*, but among all the *Prisoners* that are there, none will surprise you so much as

when

when I tell you that there is a *Cruxifx* kept
there, which is called, *our Saviour in the In-*
quisition: when this was first told me, I durst
not speak out that which naturally occur-
ed to my thoughts, which was, that our *Sa-*
viour and the *Truth of his Gospel*, was indeed
hut up with so much severity by the *Inquisi-*
ors, that it was no wonder if he were recko-
ed among the *Prisoners* of that severe Court.
But this story is less serious, and more Comical.

Youknow that in all the bigotted *Towns*,
he *people* are sorted in several *Fraternities*,
ad every one of these, has their peculiar
churches, *Altars*, *Images* and *Relicks*, to
which they pay a more extraordinary devo-
on: so there was one in *Florence*, among
*those favourite *Images* a *Crucifix* hapned to
e one: a *Woman* (that had a fair *Daughter*)
ll sick: and as she had payed many Devo-
ons to that *Image*, so she came to fancy,
*at in her sickness she had the Returns of
ry extraordinary Favours from it. The
uth of the matter was, that one who had a
ind to have frequent access to her *Daugh-*
r, made a shift to deceive the poor *sick*
oman: for he appeared in such a disguise
her, that she believed it was the *Image*
at came to comfort her. And that which
as the most acceptable part of the Impo-
ure was, that the *Impostor* knew by her
aughters means, every thing that she wan-
G 2   ted,

ted , and took care to provide it for her
so that at every visit that he made her , h
brought along with him , all the things tha
she needed: this was sensible ; so the credulou
Woman believed all this came from her be
loved *Image*: and she was now as gratefull a
she had been before devout : she told all tha
came to see her ; how careful and bountifu
that *Image* was to her: and shewed ther
how well she was supplied by it. In shor
this came to be generally believed : for whe
the least *story* of this kind gets vent, and
well received by the *Priests*, the *People* ru
in so headlong to it, that it would pass fc
a Crime capable enough of ruining one in th
Spirit of the *Inquisitors* , to seem to doul
of it; but much more if one studied to unde
ceive others: therefore things of this natu
kindle the minds of a superstitious multitud
so quick, that in a few days a whole *Tou*
will seem as it was out of its Wits : whic
appeared signally on this occasion at *Florenc*
for now the whole *Town* entred into this *Fr*
ternity. The *Great Duke* himself came in:
the number , and all were studying what ne
Honours should be done to an *Image* that h
been so kind to one of its *Worshippers*. But son
that were wiser than the rest, saw thro tl
Cheat, and Informed *P. Innocent* the 10th.
it, who was resolved to put a stop to the cu
rent of this *Superstition* : yet he saw it wasn
                                    cessa

ceffary to do it with fome addrefs: It fell out
to be the year of *Iubily* 1650. fo the *Pope* writ
to *Florence*, that he had heard of the *Miracles*
of that *Image*, to which he defired earneftly to
do his own *Devotions*, therfore he intreated
them to bring it to *Rome*; that fo the *Image*
might have the addreffes of all the *Pilgrims*, as
well as his own made to it. Upon this the
more bigotted of the *Fraternity*, would needs
accompany the Charitable *Image* : fo they
carried it in *Proceffion* to *Rome* : and did not
doubt but that the *Pope* and *Cardinalls* with
the *Clergy* of *Rome* would have come out in *Pro-*
ceffion to meet them and their *Image* : The fur-
prife was no doubt very great, when inftead of
all this, they found a Company of *Sbirri* ftaying for them at the *Porta dell Populo* ; who
took their *Image* from them, and carried it
away to the *Inquifition*; and fent them away
or a little mortified at the Difgrace, that
had befallen their *Crucifix*, who has been
ever fince a *Prifoner* in the *Inquifition*.

I was told of another *Prifoner* there of a
later date, but not much unlike this. You
know the legend of the *Plague* that was in
Rome, as I remember in S. *Gregory the great's*
time, that was ftopt by an *Angel*, that as was
pretended came down, and ftood over that
Caftle, which was formerly called *Moles Ha-*
driani, but has carried the name of *Caftro S.*
Angelo ever fince. The *Fryers* of *Ara Cœli* had
G 3 got

got a *Stone*, upon which there was an Im
preffion like the print of a *Foot*: fo they ha
put this in fome part of their *Church*, and
gave it out that this print was made by th
Foot of that *Angel*; tho one can *hardly* Ima
gine how they fancied that an *Angel* treads f
hard. This *Stone* had many *Devotions* paye
it. The learned Sig^{r.} *Pietro Bellori*, who
without difpute the beft *Antiquary* in *Rome*
being once in that *Chappel* at his Devotions
obferved a great many praying about th
Stone, and kiffing it with great Refpect ar
Affection; fo he came to look upon it, ar
having examined it carefully, he faw clea
ly it was a fragment of a Statue of the Godde
Ifis; the *Greek* Characters were legible, ar
many things concurred to make a man of l
Learning and Exactnefs conclude, that t
Devotions were mis-applied that were pay
it; fo he went to one of the *Fathers* of t
Houfe, and acquainted him with his Obferv
tion: and wifhed that they would remo
that miftaken Object of Worfhip, left for
of the learned *Hereticks* that paffed thro *Ron*
might difcover and reproach the *Church* w
it. But the *Fathers* of the *Houfe* found th
account in this matter, fo they were fo
from following his good Advice, that th
afperfed him that had given it, fo as to acc
him of Impiety for diverting the Devotic
of the people: the Imputation was carried

far that he was brought before the *Inquifition* to clear himfelf, which he did fo fully, that he not only got fafe out of their hands, but which was more, he convinced them that he was in the right: fo the *Stone* was removed, and keeps the *Crucifix* company in the *Inqui-fition*.

But by thefe two Storys, you will perhaps magin that I defign to beget in you a good Opinion of that *Court*; but I will now tell you another, that will foon bring you back o your old thoughts of that Tribunal. *Burrhi* s a man fo famous in the World, that one hat has looked into Natural *Philofophy* and *Chimiftry*, could not be long in *Rome* with-ut making an acquaintance with him: but o tell you truth, I neither found him to e fo great a *Chimift* as he fancies himfelf to e, nor fo great a *Heretick* as the *Inquifitors* ave made him. I tell you this the more par-cularly, that you may upon it judge how r you are to believe the account that the *Inquifitors* may give of their proceedings a-ainft *Molinos*: fince you may conclude from hat was done to the *one*, what may be ex-ected in all cafes that are brought before hem. *Burrhi*'s Story is in fhort this; He is a *Gentleman* of the *Millanefe*, who was born o an Eftate of 8000. *Crowns* a year: In his outh he had travelled, and had got into his ead the Notions of the *New Philofophy* and

G 4 of

of *Chimiſtry*: ſo at his return to *Milan*, he began to propogate the *new Philoſophy*, and to form a Conference upon thoſe matters: the *Prieſts* it ſeems ſuſpected, that there might be ſomewhat under this, ſo he was put in the *Inquiſition*, but nothing could be made out againſt him, he was let out: after that he went and ſtayd for ſome years in *Germany* and *Holland*; and it is very probable that he might have expreſſed himſelf concerning the *Courts* of *Inquiſition*, as a man that had no great opinion either of their Juſtice, or of their Mercy. And as he has gone into all the high pretenſions of the *Chimiſts*, ſo it is probable enough that he has talked of matters of *Religion* in that Myſterious unintelligible *Jargon*, that is uſed almoſt by all the men that are of the higheſt Elevation of *Chimiſtry*, but chiefly by *Paracelſus* and *Van Helmont*. In ſhort, ſome Accuſations were given in to the *Inquiſitors* againſt him, who complained of him to the *Emperour*, and had ſo much credit in his *Court* that he ſtrained his power to the utmoſt, and ſeiſed on him, and ſent him to *Italy*, where thoſe good *Fathers* were reſolved not to give him a ſecond occaſion of boaſting, that he had got ſafe out of their hands: ſtrange things were objected to him;. and as is pretended, they were proved againſt him; as that the *B. Virgin was God equal with the Son; and that the H. Ghoſt was incarnate in her,*

her, *as well as the Eternal Word was in her Son: that the three Persons in the Trinity were* the firſt, *the* ſecond, *and the* third *Heavens: that the Son was from all Eternity diſcontented with the Father, for not making him equal to him: that the Conſecrated Hoſty had in it the Body of the Mother as well as that of the Son: and that the putting the pieces of it together in the Chalice, demonſtrated the Union between the Mother and the Son.* Theſe Opinions were all proved againſt him: tho he proteſts that he never thought of them, yet he was forced to abjure them in the year 1668. and was upon that condemned to perpetual Impriſonment; he continued in the Priſon of the *Inquiſition,* till within theſe five or ſix years, that the Duke *d'Eſtrees* being ſick, procured an Order for having *Burrhi* to come and treat him; and in gratitude to *Burrhi,* who cured him, he got his Priſon changed to the Caſtle St. *Angelo:* where he now entertains himſelf with *Chimical* Proceſſes. It is indeed very probable, that he had provoked the *Inquiſition,* by ſpeaking ſeverely and reproachfully of them, and this was all his Crime, unleſs another *Article* againſt him might be his *Eſtate;* for of his 8000. *Crowns* a year, there is but 3000. left him; for the good *Fathers* have had the Charity to take 5000. to themſelves: and his 3000. is ſo eat up by them, thro whoſe hands it comes to him, that he has not 1500.

G 5 *Crowns*

Crowns a year payed him : and from this you may see what credit you ought to give to the *Proceffes*, the *Articles* , and the *Abjurations* that are made before that *Court*.

If inftead of that Zeal which animates them againft *Herefy*, they would purge their own *Church* of thofe Diforders , which they themfelves acknowledg to be corruptions, they would fooner bring themfelves again into credit. The fcandalous *Pictures* that are in many *Churches* of *Italy*, are things that might deferve their care, if they would turn it to that hand. Is it not a fhameful thing, that there has not been a great *Mafter* in *Painting* who has not put that Complement on his *Miftrefs*, as to paint her for the *Virgin?* fo that the moft celebrated *Madonna's* of *Italy* are known to have been the *Miftreffes* of the Great *Painters*. The *Poftures*, the *Looks*, and the *Nakednefs* of many of the *Church-pieces*, are Monftrous Indecent things. The great defign of the *Cupulo* at *Florence*, is fuch a Reprefentation of *Vice*, that all that can be prefented by a defiled Imagination, comes fhort of what is to be feen there: and tho the *Scripture* fpeaks but of one Apparition of the *Holy Ghoft* in the fhape of a *Dove*; one fhall find this Dove on the Head, at the Ear, and the Mouth of I know not how many of their *Saints*; and as one finds in many *Pieces*, that their *Mafters* have refolved to perpetuate
their

their own Amours in them, fo Amours are every day managed by the fame methods: for while I was at *Rome*, I difcovered an Intrigue between a *Fryer* and a *Nun*, by two *Pictures*, that were drawn for them : the *Fryer* was drawn as a S. *Anthony*, and the *Nun* as a S. *Katherine of Siena*: thefe they were to exchange, and fo to feed their paffion under this difguife of Devotion.

But to return to Indecent *Pictures*, there is nothing more fcandalous, than the many various Reprefentations of the *Trinity*, which muft needs give to all *Jews* and *Mahometans* as well as to *us*, that pafs for *Hereticks*, a ftrange horror to a *Religion* that fuffers thofe odious Refemblances, that give fuch grofs Ideas of the *Deity*, and of the *Trinity* : and that which is yet the moft fcandalous part of thofe *Pictures*, is that the Reprefentation of *God the Father* is often diverfified according to the caprice of the Painter; and he is to be feen in the Habits of the feveral *Orders* of that *Church*, and indeed both Features, Hair, Habit, and Poftures, have all the diverfity in them that is neceffary to feed an *Idolatry*, that is as Extravagant as it is grofs.

The Picture of the B. *Virgin*, with the *Order* of the *Capuchins* under her Petticoat, is not very apt to raife Chaft Idea's in thofe who look upon it. In fhort, whereas the Rule of the Antient *Architecture* of *Churches*, was to

be

below and dark, which was thought the most proper, for the Recollection of a man's Faculties, and by consequence for *Devotion*, is now quite altered: and great *Cupulos* with a vast Illumination, are necessary to shew the Beauty of those rich Pieces, which would be lost in *Churches* built as dark as the Antient Ones were.

I confess, those Pictures are charming things, if they were any where else than in *Churches*: but the pleasure they give, does so possess a man that begins to understand them, that it will kindle any thoughts in him, sooner than devout ones. I will not here let my Pen carry me into a Subject that must needs set all my thoughts on fire; and speak of the great *Pieces* of *Painting* that are in *Italy*, and of the many *Masters* that it produced in the last Age: who as they were such Extraordinary men, so they lived within the Compass of one Age; as if the Perfection in that amasing Art had been to dye with them, as well as it was born with them; this, I say, would make one think, that there are Revolutions and Aspects in the Heavens that are favorable or cross to Arts or Sciences: and that then, the most favourable Aspect for *Painting* that ever was, produced those astonishing performances. For tho the great decay of Learning that is every where, may be reasonably enough resolved in this, that whereas in the
last

laſt *Age* many great *Princes* were either *Learn-ed* themſelves , or at leaſt they made it a Maxim to protect and encourage *Learning*; but this having at laſt grown to an exceſs of Rudeneſs and Pedantry , and Princes beco-ming generally extream Ignorant, it came to paſs for a piece of breeding, to ſay nothing that was beyond their pitch , or that ſeemed to reproach their Ignorance : and thoſe who could not hide their Learning , were called *Pedants*: and pedantry was repreſented ſo odious, that Ignorance being the laſieſt as well as the ſureſt way to avoid this, all men took that very naturally; and when other methods are as effectual to raiſe men to the higheſt preferments either of the *Barr* or of the *Pulpit* as true Learning or reall Merit, few will chooſe the long and tedious, and often the moſt uncertain way, when the End that they propoſe to themſelves , may be cer-tainly compaſſed by a more effectual and ea-ſier one. Flattery and Submiſſions are ſooner Learned and eaſier practiſed by men of low and mean ſouls , than much hard and dry ſtudy : thus, I ſay, the decay of *Learning* is very eaſily accounted for, in the *Age* in which we live : but as for the Art of *Painting* , it is ſtill in ſuch eſteem , and great pieces go ſtill at ſuch vaſt rates , that if the Genius and capacity for it were not loſt , there is encouragment enough ſtill to ſet it a going:
but

but I leave this fubject not without putting
fome conftraint on my felf; for who can think
of fuch Wonderful men as *Correge*, *Michael
Angelo*, *Raphael*, *Paulo Veronefe*, *Iulio Ro-
mano*, *Carrache*, *Palma*, *Titian* and *Tintoret*,
without feeling a concern at every time that
he reflects on the Wonders of their pencils:
St. *Lukes* pretended work, and even the fuppofed performances of *Angels*, are fad things
fet near their *pieces*. One, whofe thoughts are
full of the Wonders of that *Art*, that are to
be feen in *Florence*, goes into the *Annunciata*,
and fees not without Indignation, that ado-
red *picture* of the *Virgin*, which, as the fond
people there believe, was finifhed by an *Angel*, while the *Painter* that was working at it,
and that could not animate it as he defired,
fell afleep, who as foon as he awaked, faw
his piece finifhed. This fiction of the *painters*,
to raife the credit of his *picture*, is fo well believed at *Florence*, that the *prefents* made to
enrich the *Altar* and *Chappel*, where it ftands,
are Invaluable:& yet after all, the *Angel's* work
is ftill no better than the common *painting* of
that time: and that *Angel-painter*, was but a
bungler if compared, to the great *Mafters*. In
a word, what can be thought of humane nature, when in fo refined a place as *Florence*,
fo courfe an Impofture has been able to
draw to it, fuch an Ineftimable ftock of
Wealth.

All

All thefe things are fo many digreffions from my main fubject, which was, to shew you how much matter the *Inquifitors* might find, if they would ufe any exactnefs in redrefling thofe Abufes which they themfelves will not defend in common converfation: and yet tho the fmalleft thing, that feems even at the greateft diftance to go againft their Intereft, is lookt after with a very watchful care; yet the groffeft of all Impoftures, that proves profitable to them, is much encouraged by them.

The fable of *Loretto*, is fo black and fo ridiculous a piece of Impofture, that I never faw a man offenfe, that cared to enter upon that fubject. I was once in Company where I took the liberty to propofe two modeft Exceptions to it: the one was, that about 200 *years* after the reft of the Angelical Labour in carying about that *Cottage* is pretended to have fallen out, *Vincent Ferrier*, whom they believe a great Saint, not only fayes nothing of its being then in *Italy*, but fayes exprefly, that it was then in *Nazareth*, & that many *Miracles* were wrought about it. *Antonin* of *Florence*; who is alfo the moft Impudent Writer of *Legends* that ever was, fay's not a word of it fome Ages after they fay that it was at *Loretto*. All the anfwer that I had to this was, that it was no Article of Faith, but whether it was true or falfe, the Devotion

tion of the People was still entertained by it: and this, they said, was as much meritorious, tho founded on a Fable, as the giving of Charity to one who is believed a fit object, but yet is indeed a Cheat, is acceptable to God: and thus he who gives upon a good inward motive, will be rewarded according to the Difposition of his Mind, and not according to the Truth or Falfehood of the *Story*, that wrought upon him. I durst not prefs this matter too far: otherwife I would have replied, that how excufeable foever the Superftition of Ignorant *People* may be, yet this does not at all juftify the Cheat that the *Church* puts upon her fo eafily deluded children. The truth is, the *Romans* themfelves have not fuch ftiff notions of all the points of *Controverfy* as we are apt to Imagine: this makes me remember a converfation that paft fome years ago, between an *Abbot* & one of our *Clergymen*, that was then a Governour to a *Perfon* of Quality, that in his *Travels* ftayed for fome time at *Rome*. The *Abbot* feeing the *Governour* was confidered as a man of *Learning*, defired to be Informed of him, what were the *Points* in difference between the *two* Churches: fo the Governour told him, that *we* had our *worship* in a known tongue; that we gave the *Cup* in the Sacrament; that we had no *Images*, and did not pray to *Saints*: all this did not difturb the *Abbot*, who faid, that thefe were only
diffe-

different *Rites* and *Ceremonies* , which might be well enough born with : when the other added, that we did not believe *Tranfubftan-tiation* nor *Purgatory* , the *Abbot* faid, thefe were the fubtilties of the School : fo he was very gentle till the *Governour* told him , that we did not acknowledge the *Pope* ; then the *Abbot* was all on fire, and could not comprehend, how men could be *Chriftians* , that did not acknowledge Chrifts *Vicar* , and S. *Peter's Succeffor* : and it is very plain at *Rome* at this day , that they confider the *Converfion* of *Nations* , only as it may bring in more profit into the *Datary Court*, and raife the value of the *Offices* there ; for when I feemed amafed in converfation with fome of them , to fee fo little regard had to the *Ambaffadour* of *England* , and to every thing that he propofed ; they told me plainly, that perhaps the Angels in Heaven rejoiced at the converfion of a finner upon the pure motives of perfect Charity , but they at *Rome* looked at other things. They faw no *profit* like to come from *England* ; no *Bulls* were called for, and no *Compofitions* like to be made ; if thofe things fhould once appear, then an *Ambaffadour* from thence would be treated like the penitent Prodigal , efpecially if he were a little lefs governed by the *Jefuites*, who were believed to have managed our *Ambaffadour* a little too abfolutely : and here it will be no unpleafant digreffion if I tell you

H the

the true reafon that retarded the *Promotion* of the Cardinal *d'Efté* fo long.

The *Pope* himfelf faw what the *Uncle* of this *Cardinal* did at *Rome*, in P. *Alexander* the 7th s time, upon the bufinefs of the *Corfis*, and the affront that was put on the Duke of *Crequy*, which made fo much noife. That *Cardinal* being then the *Protector* of the *French Nation*, offered firft to the D. of *Crequy*, to go with him, accompanied with 500 Men, that he knew he could raife in *Rome*, to the Palace of *Dom Mario Chigi*, and to fling him out at window: but the D. of *Crequy* thinking that fuch a revenge went too far, the *Cardinal* himfelf went accompanied with his 500 Men to the *Palace*, and expoftulated the matter with the *Pope*, and demanded Reparation; and when the *Pope* put it by in fome general an-fwers, he preft him fo hard, till the *Pope* threat-ned to pull his *Cap* from him, but he anfwered, *that he would clap a Head-piece on it, to defend it, and that he would never part with that, till he had pulled the Tripple Crown from his head :* This was vigorous, and the *Cardinal* had a mind to perpetuate the memory of it, for he made himfelf be drawn with a *Headpiece* by him, his hand pointing towards it, which I faw at *Modena*; and it is plain by their way of fpea-king of this matter, that they were proud of it The prefent *Pope* being at that time a *Cardinal* faw this diforder, and fo he was refolved never
to

to raife one of that *family* to the *Purple*: yet the earneft and repeated Inftances from *England,* overcame him at laft.

But now again I return to that from which I have digreffed fo often, which is the work that the *Inquifition* might find in *Italy*, even without departing from any of their received Principles. That fcandalous Impofture of the *blood* of S. *January* at *Naples*, that feems to be firm & dry in the *Vial*, and that diffolves and moves as it is brought near his Head, which is fo firmly believed by all the bigots there, muft needs give an Indignation to all that love Truth, when they fee fuch grofs Deceptions put upon the World. I will not take upon me to fay how it is managed; but nothing is more eafy than the ordering of this matter may be. For if that *Vial* be filled with tinctured liquor, the *Vial* being put in Ice and Salt, will freefe in an Inftant; and it being again in the air, may return very quickly to its former ftate, fo that there is no need of any great skill for the conducting this matter: and it is fo much their Intereft, who have the keeping of this pretended *Blood,* to keep the fecret very religioufly, that it is no wonder if it is not difcovered. He indeed who either doubts of it, or would adventure to difcover it, muft refolve to go and live fome were elfe than in *Naples*, where this paffes for the chief Glory, as well as the greateft blef-fing of their *City*: and the *people* there are fo

ex-

extreamly credulous, & the *Priests* are so very
Insolent, that this has appeared of late in such
Instances, that if the *Viceroy* of *Naples*, were
not both a very extraordinary man, and most
excessively esteemed and beloved there, he
could not have stood his ground in the *Dispute*
which is now on foot, and of which tho all the
Gazettes make mention , yet I may perhaps
tell you some particulars, that may be new to
you, for I was in *Naples* while this matter was
in its greatest heat.

The business of the *Ecclesiastical Immunities*
is carried so high here, that the *General* of the
Horse, who is by birth a *Flemming*, had almost
felt it to his cost ; there were two under him
that had quarrelled, but were made Friends
and one of these meeting the other some days
after that, he embraced him with all the shewe
of Friendship, but having a *stiletto* in his hand
he managed it so fatally, that under all the ap
pearences of tender Embraces, he killed him
out-right, and presently he took Sanctuary in
a *Church*, that was hard by ; the *General* hear
ing of this, resolved he would make an Exam
ple of the *Murderer* : but not daring to drag
him out of the *Church*, he set a Sentinel to the
Doors, reckoning that hunger would soon
force him to come out: and tho the *Priest*
that belonged to the *Church*, carried him in
some Provisions, yet that could not serve him
long. But the General was forced to discharg
he

the *Sentinels*: for he was Informed, that an *Excommunication* was coming out againſt him, for diſtrurbing the devotions of thoſe that went to the *Church*: and he knew that if the *Excommunication* ſhould be once given out, nobody would ſo much as talk with him or come near him after that: ſo he would not run that riſque: and this *Aſſaſſinate* had a fair occaſion given him to make his eſcape: this was a good Eſſay of the Zeal for the *Immunity of places*. Another fell out about the ſame time near *Leghorn*, in which the ſacredneſs of exempted *perſons* was aſſerted in a manner that was no leſs ſcandalous; a *Prieſt* was ſeiſed on, for a moſt horrid Crime, either a *Rape or a Murder*, I do not remember which: but he who had no mind to be taken, defended himſelf; and ſhot one of the *Sbiri*, upon which the reſt run away. So he apprehending that a ſtronger party would be ſent, that would be too hard for him, went and retired into a Wood, with his Fuſee; and ſome being ſent to find him out, he had *ſhot* ſix or ſeven of them; yet after all the ſacred Character was like to ſave this execrable man; for while I was at *Leghorn* I was told that an *Excommunication* was coming out, againſt all that ſhould violate the *Eccleſiaſtical Immunities* in his Perſon: and no doubt the *Great Duke* will give way to this: for he is ſo entirely delivered up to his *Prieſts*, and is become ſo

ex-

exceffively fcrupulous, that to deliver himfelf from thofe Troubles of Confcience , which many things , in the Adminiftration of the *Government* are apt to give him, he has found out an eafy receipt, which if all other *Princes* can be brought to follow, it will be very happy for their *Minifters*. He then confiders, that the only fure way to be Innocent in the Conduct of Affairs, is not to know them at all : but to devolve them entirely on his *Minifters*, who do all, without fo much as communicating matters to him.

But the *Viceroy* of *Naples* is not fo very tractable in thofe matters , as appears by the vigour with which he has fupported the *fecular Tribunal* againft the Invafions of the *Ecclefiaftical Court*.   That which gave the rife to the difpute , was, a *fute* that was between a *Layman* and a *Church-man* , before one of the *Judges* of *Naples*, who decided in favour of the *Layman* ; upon which it was pretended, that this was a Violation of the *Immunities* of the *Church*: fo the *Judge* was *Excommunicated*; And upon it no body would willingly appear before him, or fo much as fpeak to him, fo terrible a thing is that Thunder there : but the *Viceroy* has fhewed on this occafion, that firmnefs that has appeared in all his other Actions : and has alfo received *Orders* from *Spain* authorifing him to keep his ground.   The *Judge* is not only maintained in what he has done , but continues ftill to fit on the *bench*, all people are

forced

forced to bring their caufes before him; & his
Sentences are executed with refolution. This
Contempt put on the *Ecclefiaftical* Cenfures
by a *Minifter* of *Spain*, and at a time in which
the *Pope* is fo much in their *Interefts*, is a little
Extraordinary. But the affront that the *Viceroy* put on an *Auditor* of the *Nuntio's*, was
yet much more provoking, for it was managed
with a particular care to make the Scorn very
wounding as well as it was publick. The *Nuntio* is believed to do ill Offices in this matter;
and his *Auditor* was known to be a man of *Liberties*; it was found out that he went often to
a *Bordello*; the *Viceroy* therefore gave order to
watch him fo carefully, that the *Sbiri* fhould
be fure to find him in fuch circumftances, as
fhould make his fhame very Confpicuous: fo
he was taken, and carried before the next
Judge: the thing was laid beforehand, and the
Judge refufing to medle in it, the *Sbiri* (a fort
of men like our *Bailiffs*) carried him to another, and fo made the round of all the *Judges*
in *Naples*; and every one of them refufing to
medle with the *Auditor*, the *Sbiri* let him go,
when the matter was made fufficiently publick, by their carrying him about to fo man-
ny places. The *Nuntio* complained of the Violation of the Rights of a *Publick Minifter*, e-
fpecially of fo facred a one. But the Reparation
that the *Viceroy* made, was a redoubling of
the Affront: for he ordered the *Sbiri* that had

taken

taken the *Auditor*, to be carried about all *Naples* with an *Inscription* writ in Capital Letters, both on their Breasts and on their Backs, mentioning the Crime for which they were thus led about, *which was their having disturbed the Nuntio's Auditor in his pleasures.*

You will easily imagin that this was considered at *Rome* as a most outrageous Affront; and indeed the *Pope* has carried the matter of the *Regale* in *France* so very far, that it is hard to tell to what a degree this breach in *Naples* may be also carried: for tho the *Pope* is most excessively ignorant in all those Matters, yet he has another Quality, that is the only thing that is great in him, and that would indeed become him very well, if he had a little more Knowledg to govern it: and that is, *that he is the wilfullest man alive*; and his temper is fearless enough to make him shut his Eyes upon all Danger.

It cannot be denied, but it is the Interest of the *Pope*, as he is a *Temporal Prince*, to be of the side that is now the weakest; and that needs his support the most: and therefore it is no wonder if he is so favourable to the Crown of *Spain*, and the House of *Austria*: but after all, his carrying the business of the *Regale* so far, against so great a *King*, and a *King* that has merited so much from that *Church*, by his zeal against *Hereticks*, is

some-

fomewhat unaccountable: After all the Ha-
vock, that has been made both by *Princes*
and *Popes* of the true Liberties of the *Church,*
and particularly after that fhameful Bargain
that was made between them in the *Concor-
date*, it has a very ill grace to fee a *Pope* make
this the fubject of fo great and fo long a Difpute; and that the factious Clamours of a
few ill-natured and angry *Priefts*, fhould
have been fo much confidered, as to interrupt the good underftanding of the *Courts* of
the *Vatican* and *Verfailles*. All this flowed
from the ill opinion that the *Pope* had of the
Jefuites, which being known in *France*, the
Janfenifts thought it was high time for them
to recommend themfelves to the *Court* of
Rome, in hope of mortifying the *Jefuites:*
yet they could not with any decency carry
the *Papal Authority* high, after they had
with fo much force both of reafon and learning, depreffed it as they had done: fo they
betook themfelves to the firft thing that offered it felf, that they knew would be very
acceptable in *Rome*, which was the afferting
the *Liberties* of the *Church*, and the difpu-
ting the *Kings* Impofing the *Rights* of the
Regale (that is, the mean profits of *Bifhopricks*,
and the *Collating* to *Benefices* without *Cure*,
during the Vacancy) on the four fouthern
Provinces of *France*. I will not fay more of
a matter that is fo well known, only I will tell

H 5   you.

you, what a *Doctor* of the *Sorbon* said to me
upon this subject; I found he did not believe
the *Pope's Authority* more than I did my self;
and yet he was one of those that indirectly op-
posed the *Articles* of the *Clergy*, and the condemnation that was past on the Bishop of
Strigonium's Censure of those *Articles*; for
his Authority and Learning gave a great turn
to that matter: so when I seemed amased at
this, that a man of his Principles, had acted
as he had done upon that occasion, he told me,
he had no other Consideration before him in
that matter, but to mortify the *Clergy* of
France, and to maintain the Dignity of the
Sorbon. It was not long since that in the Dispute about *Jansenius's* matter, they had
made the *Pope* not only *Infallible* in matters
of *Right*, but of *Fact*: and now because the
Pope was not in the Interests of *France*, the
dispute of *Infallibility*, and of the Councils
of *Constance* and *Basil*, were again set on foot;
all which would be given up, and the *Pope*
would be considered *Infallible* to morrow, if
he were once more in the Interests of *France*; &
the *Clergy*, who had neither learning nor vertue,
but made up all Defects, by a slavish Obsequi-
ousness, would be then as forward to magnify
the *Infallibility*, as they are now to depress it.

How far the *Pope* will embroil himself in
this new business of the *Franchises*, I do not
know: he has expressed a great steadiness in
it;

it; and the truth is, *Rome* is now so sunk
from what it was, and the *Franchises* are so
considerable a part of the City, that their
being covered from the *Execution*, both of
Civil and Criminal *Justice*, is a most horrible
Disorder : and it seems reasonable enough,
that as in all other Courts, there is nothing
now under the *Ambassadours* Protection, but
that which is within his Gates, so the same
Regulation should be made in *Rome*; where
the extent of those priviledged Places is very
great : yet after all, if the *French Ambassadour*,
that is now on his way thither, has positive
Orders to maintain them, and has mony e-
nough to list men, if the matter goes on to a
more obstinate Dispute; It will be no hard
matter for him to raise such a Revolt in *Rome*,
that neither the *Popes Guards*, nor those in the
Castle of St. *Angelo*, will be able to subdue
it : and if this matter goes on so far, the
French will very probably cut off all *Annates*,
and find a shorter way of granting of *Bulls*
within the *Kingdom*. It is said, that while some
have represented the apparent Inconveniences
of a Rupture with *France* to the *Pope*, and
that he was in no condition to resist that mighty Power : He answered, *that he would suffer Martyrdom in maintaining the Rights of*
St. *Peter*. It must be confessed, that there
was something in this saying that was
more Magnanimous, than prudent. And indeed

deed the *Popes* way of {treating with *Am-baſſadours*, has ſomewhat in it that comes, neerer the ſimplicity of the Fiſhermen, the more modern Politicks. His dry Anſwer to our *Ambaſſadour*, when he threatned him that he would leave *Rome*, and go back to *England*, if he were not better uſed; *Lei e Padrone*; *You are Maſter of that as you pleaſe*; had an air in it that I ſhould have been much pleaſed with, if it had fallen on any other than on the *King's Miniſter.*

His Conduct of the *Revenue* is an unac-countable thing; for if there is not a vaſt *Treaſure* laid up, or a moſt prodigious deal of *Wealth* ſecretly conveyed to his *Family*, it is not to be imagined what has become of all that *Revenue* that he has raiſed, in which the Income is ſo vaſtly diſproportioned to the ex-pence, that the moſt prying men do not know what is become of it. The War with the *Turks* has not coſt him ſo much as is believed; on the contrary, many think that he has got by it; and that the *Taxes* which he has laid on the *Clergy* of *Italy* amount to more than he has laid out upon it: It is certain, it has not coſt him very much. He retrenched all Ex-pences to ſo great a degree, that even the pu-blick *Charities* were leſſened: for in *Lent*, there is a weekly Charity of a *Julio*, or a ſix pence, to all the *poor* that come and ask it: and the poor commonly brought their Children with
                                   them,

them, fo that they got as many *Julio's* as
they brought *Children*; but the *Pope* limited
this, that no Charity fhould be given to any
under fuch an Age, as I remember it was below ten year old. The Adminiftration of the
Revenue is indeed the only thing that he un-
derftands, and in which he imploys all his
thoughts : and it was believed, that the true
Secret of the greateft number of the *Cardi-*
nals in the laft *Promotion*, was the Advantages
that he made by the fale of the *Offices* which
they held, and that fell to the *Pope* upon their
Advancement; out of which it was thought
that he gained above a *Million*: and upon
this I will tell you, what I have learned concerning the averfion that two of the *Cardinals,*
Taia and *Ricci*, expreffed to the *Purple* in the
Promotion that was made five year ago; this
was magnified in feveral Books, that were
printed out of *Italy*, as fomewhat that feemed
to approach to the beft Ages of the Primitive
Times, when men refufed to accept of fo
great a *Dignity*, that brought them within a
ftep of the *Supream Elevation* : but the truth
of this matter was, they were both men of
Fourfcore, and not like to live long; as they
both died within a year of their Preferment :
they had very good Imployments, which
they had bought, and which by their accepting the *Purple* were to fall into the *Popes*
hands : befides that, the new *Dignity* was not
                                            to

to be entred upon without a great Expence : so all this being considered, the vertue of refusing so chargeable a *Dignity*, in men that were more concerned for their *Families*, than for that small remnant of life that was before them, was not so very Extraordinary.

But since I am upon the discourse of *promoting* of *Cardinals*, I will tell you a remarkable Instance of a *Promotion*, that I do not remember to have met with in any *Book*; and the Dignity of the *Person* and of the *Family* descended from him makes me think it worth the relating; and the rather because I had it from no ordinary person, but from one of the exactest men in *Rome*, and who has taken the greatest pains to be well Informed in the *Modern History*. I had seen several pictures of *Clara Farnese*, for there are more than one of them in the *Palestrina* : so I knowing nothing concerning her, asked her story, which in short was this : that she was P. *Paul* the 3*d's Sister*, and the person to whom he owed his *Cardinals Cap*; and by Consequence all that followed upon it, tho he rewarded her ill for it; for he *poysoned* both *her* and his *Mother*, that he might have all their Wealth; their *Father* was a poor man, that went about selling *Saucidges* and such sort of stuff. *Clara* was married young, and was soon a *Widdow*; she was a lovely woman, but no Extraordinary beauty : her *Brother* was bred to Letters, and was one of those

poor

poor *Churchmen,* that was looking about on all hands where he might find a Patron; when of a sudden his *Sisters* charms and her artifices together raised him to a height, to which he was far enough from pretending at that time. On a great occasion *Clara Farnese* was so near P. *Alexander* the 6th, and was so much in his Eye & in his thoughts, that he ordered one that was about him, to enquire who she was, and where she lived: Instruments upon such occasions are never wanting to great Persons: and notwithstanding the *Popes* great Age, yet his Vices hung still so close to him, that he could have no quiet till *Clara Farnese* was brought him. She resolved to manage her self on this occasion, and to raise her price all that was possible, so a *Cardinals Cap* to her Brother was both asked and granted: a promise of it was made at least, upon which she came and attended on the old leud *Pope*: yet when the next *Promotion* came to be in agitation, the Proposition for *Abbot Farnese* was rejected by *Cesar Borgia* with scorn; he had never been a slave to his word, and he had no mind that his *Father* should observe it on this occasion.

The way of a *Promotion* is this, the *Pope* setles the *List* of the *Cardinals*, and writes down all their names in a paper with his own hand; and in a *Consistory,* when all other business is ended, he throws down the *Paper* on the Table, and say's to the Cardinals, *habetis Fratres*;

you

you have now some Brethren. One of the *Secretaries* upon that takes up the Paper, and reads the *Names* aloud; and the *Sbiri* are at the door, and as soon as one is named, they run for it, to see who shall be able to carry the first newes of it to the party concerned.

Upon this occasion, the *Pope* after he had concerted the *Promotion* with his *Son*, writ down all the names. *Clara Farnese* was in great apprehensions for her *Brother*, so she being to pass that night with the *Pope*, rise when the old man was fast asleep, & searched his Pocket, & found the *Paper*, but her *Brothers* name was not in it: then she set her self with great care to counterfeit the *Popes hand*; and writ her *Brothers name* the first in the *List*: next morning she kept the *Pope* as long in bed as was possible; till word was brought him, that the *Consistory* was set, and that the *Cardinals* were all come: for she reckoned that the less time that the *Pope* had for being drest, there was the less Danger of his looking into his *Paper*: So without ever opening it, he went into the *Consistory*, and according to Custom, he threw down the *list* on the Table: but to the great surprise of him, and of all that were upon his Secrets, the first name that was read, was that of *Abbot Farnese*; and it seems the *Pope* thought it better to let the matter pass, than to suffer the true secret of the business to break out. It is well that the Doctrine of the Intention

tion, does not belong to the Creation of *Cardinals*, otherwise here was a Nullity with a Witness. Thus begun that long course of P. *Paul* the *thirds* greatness, who lived above 50 *years* after this, and laid the Foundation of the Family of *Parma*, which he saw quite overthrown, his *Son* being assassinated in his own time; and both his *Grand-children* having revolted against him, which, as was believed, precipitated his death, tho he was then *Fourscore*.

But now I return to the present *Pope*; for I have writ you a very loose sort of a *Letter*, all made up of digressions. His aversion to the *Order* of the *Jesuites* is very visible; for he takes all occasions to mortify them; and every thing that is proposed to him, thrives the worse for their sakes, if he believes they are concerned in it; which was given by all at *Rome*, as the true reason of the cold usage that the *English Ambassadour* found there. Indeed the *Pope* is not singular in the hard thoughts that he has of that *Order*: I never saw an Indifferent man in all *Italy*, that was of another mind: they do generally look upon them as a Coveous; Fraudulent, Intriguing, and turbulent sort of people; who can never be at quiet, unless they *reign*: who are men of no Morals, that will stick at nothing that may raise the Wealth and Power of their *Order* : and at *Rome* they do not stick to say, that all the concerns

I   cerns

cerns of the *Roman Catholick Religion* muſt needs miſcarry in *England*, becauſe the *Ieſuites* are ſo much in credit there. And indeed the Extravagantly vain *Letters* that they write to *Rome* out of *England*, are ſuch contextures of *Legends*, that ever ſince I ſaw them, I know what value I ought to put on their *Letters* that come from the *Indies* and other remote Countreys; for when they take ſo great a Liberty when the Falſehood is ſo eaſily found out what muſt me think of the *Relations* that come from places at ſuch a diſtance, that they may lie with more aſſurance & leſs hazard of diſcovery

The *Letter* that was writ in *February* laſt from *Liege* to the *Ieſuites* at *Friburg*, of which ſo many *Copies* were given, that it got to the Preſs at laſt, was a good Inſtance of their Vanity, and of the ſmall regard that they have to a *Prince*, that has as they give out, ſo much for them. Their repreſenting the *King*, a ſo concerned in the *Intereſts* of their *Order* that he eſpouſed them all as if they were his own, that he was now become a *Son of th Society*, and that he was received into a communication of the Merits of the *Order*, (the a ſhare in their Treaſure upon Earth were much more conſiderable thing, than of their Treaſure that is Inviſible,) Their ſetting ou the *Kings Zeal* for their *Religion*, in ſuch high terms, that they ſay he is reſolved to die *Martyr* rather than not to ſucceed in his de ſign fign *of changing the Religion*, and *converting the Nation:* and this at a time when the *King* was declaring himfelf fo much for *Liberty of Confcience:* and their affirming that the *King* is become bigotted to fo high a degree, as to refufe to fuffer a *Prieft* to kneel down and do the duty of a *Subject* in kiffing his Hand, and to tell him, *that he himfelf ought rather to kneel down, and to kifs his Hands:* all thefe are fuch Extravagant ftrains, that by the boldnefs of them it is Evident, that they were writ by a *Iefuite*, and my *Copy* came to me from fo good a hand, and fo near the fource, that how many Falfehoods foever may be in that *Letter*, I can affure you, it is no Im- pofture, but was really *writ* by thofe of *Liege*.

In a word, all the *Romans* have fo very ill an Opinion of the *Iefuits*, that as foon as any piece of *Newes* comes from *England*, that is not favourable to their Affairs, one finds all, from the higheft to the loweft, agree in the fame fhort reflection; *Thus it muft ever be, where the Iefuites have fuch a share in the Councils.* A man long practifed in the *Court of Rome*, told me, it was impoffible it could be otherwife, for all the chief men of that *Order* are kept teaching in their *Schools*, till they are almoft forty *years* of age; and by that means Pedantry, a difputatious and imperious humour, and a peevish littlenefs of foul, becomes natural to them, fo that an

I 2   Emi-

Eminent man here faid to me, *It was Impoffible that matters could go better than they di
in* England, *as long as the Morals and the Politicks of the* Jefuites, *and the Underftanding
and Courage of the* Irifh, *were fo much relie*
on.

But befides all thefe General Confider:
tions, there are fome things in the Conftitu-
tion of the *Order* of the *Iefuites* that giv
thofe at *Rome* reafon enough to be on the
Guard againft them.   There are two thing
peculiar to this *Order* that make it very fo
midable; the one is, that thofe who hav
made the fourth *vow* are capable of no Pr
ferment, unlefs it be to be *Cardinals*, ar
then they are indeed capable of *Bifhoprick*
In moft of the other *Orders*, every man has l.
own private Intereft, and his particul
views; fo that they are not always lookii
after the concerns of their *Order*. But
Iefuite can receive no Honour but from l.
Order, therefore he Confecrates himfelf
it, and advances the *Interefts* of the *Soci:*
with all poffible zeal, knowing that the
is no other way left him to advance his ov:
Interefts, but this.   So that Hope being o:
of the great Springs of humane Nature,
Iefuite, who hopes for nothing but from l.
Order, muft be extreamly devoted to it. E
fides this, a *Iefuite* fears nothing but fro
his *Order*: They have not a *Cardinal Pi*
                                           tecti

:e*ctor*, as the other *Orders* have , to whom
in Appeal lies from the fentence of the *Ge-*
ieral of the *Order* : but the *Iefuites* are a body
nore fhut up within themfelves ; for the
entence of the *General* is definitive, and can
iever be reviewed, no *Appeal* lying from it:
vhenfoever a *Pope* comes that dares mortify
hem, he will open a way for *Appeals* , for
ill that is done, the *General* of the *Iefuites* is
he moft Abfolute and the moft Arbitrary
overaign that is in the World.

All thefe things concur to Unite almoft
ll the feveral *Interefts* in *Rome* againft this
ociety, which yet is ftrong enough to fup-
ort it felf againft them all : they have the
Miffion generally in their hands; for the Con-
regation *de Propaganda.*, payes a fmall pen-
on of 20 *Crowns* to all the *Secular Priefts*
iat are on the *Miffion*, whereas the *Iefuites*
ear the expences of their own *Miffionaries*,
i whom they allow an 100 *Crowns* a year: &
thofe of the *Propaganda* being willing to be
.fed of a charge, accept of the *Miffionaries*
iat the *Iefuites* offer them : and they find
eir account in this. Their *Miffionaries* are
)werfully recommended, fo they are quickly
ceived into *Families*, efpecially where there
e yong *children* to be bred up, or *Eftates*
be managed : for in thefe two lies their
'ength : but they never forget their *Order*,
r which they are as fo many *Factors* every

where: and they draw vaſt Preſents from a
places to the *Houſe* that returns them the
Appointments; wheras the poor *Secular Prie*
muſt make a ſhift to live out of the ſmall a
lowance that he has from the Congregatio
de Propaganda fide, and out of what he ca
raiſe by his *Maſſes*. Therefore there is nothin
that they deſire ſo much, as to ſee *Proteſtar*
States that give a Tolerance to *Popery*, gro
once ſo wiſe as to ſhut out all the *Regulars*, an
above all the *Jeſuites*; and to admit none bt
Secular Prieſts: for the former, as they ar
ſo many *Agents*, to return all the wealth tha
they can poſſibly draw together, to the *hou*
to which they belong, ſo they are united tc
gether in one Body, under a moſt ſtrict C
bedience to their *General*, which may be ;
great a prejudice to the Peace and Security (
a *Countrey*, as the other is to its Wealth an
Abundance: on the other hand, the *Secul*
Prieſts are generally good-natured men, wh
are only ſubject to their *Biſhop*, and that hav
no deſigns upon the *Government*, nor the Cor
cerns of any *Houſe* that is in *Forreign Par*
lying upon them: ſo that ſince thoſe of tha
Communion have the full exerciſe and all th
Conſolation of their Religion from *Secul*
Prieſts, even thoſe in *Rome* it ſelf wonder at th
Error of *Proteſtant States*, who have no
Learned long ago to make this difference i
the Toleration that they allow: And one tha
ha

has been almost 50 *years* in the most refined practices of the *Court of Rome*, said to me with a very sensible concern, *how happy would we here reckon our selves, if we could have a Toleration of our Religion allowed in* England, *tho it were with an Eternal Exclusion of all Regulars and Iesuites?* and added, that if he saw good grounds for making it, he himself would go and carry the Proposition to those of the *Propaganda.*

And now I am sure, I have rambled over a great Variety of matter, and have made a shift to bring in to one place or other of this *Letter*, a great many particulars, that I could have hardly brought out in an exactness of Method, without a much greater compass of words, and a greater stifness of form : but I thought it was more natural, and by consequence, that it would be more acceptable to you, to make them follow one another, in an easy and unforced contexture. I have discoursed all these matters often over and over again since I came into *Italy :* but have read very little concerning them ; therefore there may be many things here, that I mention because they were new to me, that perhaps are no newes to those that are much more Learned than my self. I have told you all that I could gather upon these subjects from the wisest and worthiest men that

I found here : I have writ of all matters
freely to you, becaufe I am in a Countrey
where freedom of difcourfe, in matters of
State efpecially, is practifed in its utmoft
extent.

I have yet matter for another long *letter*,
in which the matters of *Religion* will have
no fhare; for I will end all thefe in this;
and therfore there is one piece of the *Super-*
ftition of *Lombardy*, that affected me too fenfibly, not to lead me to beftow a fevere cenfure upon it. I went through that Country in *October* and *November*, and was often
in great diftrefs, becaufe it was not poffible
to find a Glafs of *Wine*, that could be drunk,
all being either dead or four. At *Parma* I
waited on an Eminent *Perfon*, and lamented
to him the mifery of *Travallers*, fince no
Wine was to be found that could be drunk:
he told me, the *Natives* felt this much more
fenfibly than *Strangers* did, with whom it
was foon over, but they were condemned
to fuffer that every *year*; and tho he himfelf
had *Vineyards*, that produced much more
Wine than he could confume, yet he could
not be Mafter of a good Glafs of *Wine*, for a
great many *Months* of the year; fince all
the *people* were poffeffed with this *Superftition*,
that it was Indifpenfably neceffary to mix it
with *Water* in the *Cask*, that by this means
it drunk *dead* or *four* for fo great a part of the
year:

a Device to excuſe their own *Wine* from this hard fate : for they ſaid, it muſt needs be kept unmixed, ſince in the *Sacrament* the *Wine* muſt be pure, and is then only to be mixed with *Water*; and thus in all their *Cellars* good *Wine* is to be found, where there is not a drop any where elſe that can be drunk: one would think that this is to abuſe the Weakneſs and Credulity of the *People*, a little too groſly, when they condemn all the *laity* to drink ill *Wine*, whereas they themſelves drink it pure, which is felt more ſenſibly by the *Laity*, than the depriving them of the *Chalice*, and the engroſſing it to the *Prieſt* in the *Sacrament*. Yet the *Exciſe* that is laid on the *Wine* in *Florence*, has taught the Inhabitants a point of Wiſdom, that thoſe on the other ſide of the *Appenins* are not capable of ; for the *Exciſe* being raiſed upon all their *Wine*, the *People* who have no mind to pay *Exciſe* for *Water*, keep their *Wine* pure, ſo perhaps ſome ſuch ſeverity in the Government in *Lombardy*, may likewiſe reform them in this piece of abſurd *Superſtition*, which I felt too ſenſibly with all the effects that naturally follow the drinking of four Liquor, not to Inſiſt upon it with ſome more than ordinary concern.   H 5   But

But fince I am upon the point, of the *Arts* that the *Convents* have to live eafy, I will end this *Letter* with an account of a *Houfe* that was very Extraordinary, which I faw in my way to *Italy* thro *Bavaria*; *Etal*, an Abbey of *Benedictines*, that by its foundation is bound only to maintain an *Abbot* and 25 *Monks*. It was founded by *Lewis* Duke of *Bavaria*, that was *Emperour*: the building is not anfwerable to the Endowment, which is fo vaft, that they keep a *ftable* of 150 *horfes*, which is indeed one of the beft in *Germany*, the *horfes* are of great value, and well kept: they hunt perpetually, and live in as great an abundance of all things as the *Duke* of *Bavaria* himfelf can do; and yet thefe are *Religious men*, that are dead to the World.

I cannot forget to tell you a very beau-tifully diverfified *profpect* that we had at *Burgo*, a little *Town* in the hills of *Trent*, as we lookt out at window, We faw before us a lovely *Meadow* in all the Beauty and Pride of the *Moneth* of *May*: a little beyond that was a rifing *Bank* all covered over with *Trees* in their full verdure: beyond that the ground rife higher, and the *Trees* had not yet put out their leaves, and things lookt dead and dry, as after Harveft: and beyond that there was a huge *hill*, all covered on the top with *fnow*: fo that here we faw in one pro-fpect all the *feafons* of the *year*: upon which
one

one of the Company made this reflection, that if any *Painter* should in one *Landskip*; mix all these things, that were then in our eye, he would be thought a man of an Irregular fancy, whose designes did not agree with nature; and yet we had them all then before us. I will make no Excuses nor Compliments : for those things do not mend matters, and therefore I send you my *Letter*, such as it is, just as it has grown under my Pen : and so *Adieu*.

POSTSCRIPT.

I find I have forgot to mention one very extravagant piece of *Devotion*, to which I was a Witness at *Rome*, on the 17 of *January*, which is St. *Anthonys day*, that was the great *Father* of the Monastick *Orders*, whose Life is pretended to be writ by S. *Athanase*; all *Horses* and other Beasts of Burden are believed to be in an especial manner under his *Protection* : and the *Monks* of his *Order*, have a House near *St. Maria Maggiore*; thither all the *Horses*, *Mulets* and *Asses* of *Rome*, and all round the *City*, are brought that day to the door of the *Church*, where some *Monks* stand with a Broom in *holy water*, and sprinkle it upon them all : many *Doggs* and *Lambs*, and other favo-

favorite *Animals*, are also brought to share in this *Aspersion*: which is believed to have a most special vertue: the force of this hallowing is believed to be such, that if any should fail to bring his *Horses* thither, all the Neighbourhood would look on those that have no portion in it, as accursed *Animals*, upon whom some unlucky Accident were hanging; which is so firmly believed, that none would hire a *Horse* or a *Mulet*, that had not been so sprinkled. So that from the Popes *Horses* down to the poorest man in *Rome*, all are brought thither; but this is not all, the profitable part of this piece of Folly is, that every one brings a Present; the richer sort send Purses of *Money*; some give great Wax-Lights, all stuck full of *Testons* (a piece of 20 pence) the poorer bring either smaller pieces of *Money*, or Presents of *Wine*, *Oyl*, *Bread*, or such things as they can afford: but in a Word, no man comes empty; so that this is the Market-day of those *Monks*, in which for some *Gallons* of *Water* and *Salt*, they get more Presents, than would serve to maintain them for seven *years*: they quickly convert all that is not necessary for them into *Money*: and by this means they are vastly rich. When I saw all this, I could not but think that *men* must become first *Beasts* themselves, before things of this kind could pass upon them: but since I have

added

added this in a *Poftfcript*, rather than give my felf the trouble to make it come in pertinently into my *Letter* I will add another particular that is writ me from *Rome* the fixth of *October* 1687.

I am told, that men are now more puzled in their thoughts with Relation to the bufinefs of *Molinos* than ever.   It was Vifible that his *Abjuration* was only a pretended thing; for in effect he has abjured nothing: his party believe, that they are very numerous, not only in *Rome*, *Italy*, *Spain*, and *France*, and in all thefe parts of the world, but that they have many followers even in *America* it felf: one fees now in almoft all the *Churches* in *Rome* fome of them *praying* in corners, with their Hands and Eyes lifted up to Heaven, and all in Tears, and Sighs; which is no fmall trouble to thofe who thought they had quite routed them : but find they are not fo much quafht as it was thought they would have been by the mock Triumph that was made upon *Molinos*.   Nor do they believe a word of thofe Reports that are fpread of his Leudnefs: they fay, there was no Proof ever brought of it; and that there are many *thoufands* in *Rome*, of both fexes, that converfed much with him, who have all poffible reafon to conclude, that all thefe ftories that were given out concerning him, are Impudent Calumnies, fet about only to blaft *Him* and his

Do-

Doctrine: and the truth is , this seems to be much confirmed by the *Bull* that condemns his *Books* , and his *Doctrine* ; in which no mention is made of his ill *Life* and *Hypocrisy*, which had been very probably done if the matter had been well proved : since this would not only have satisfied people , with relation to him , but would have very much confirmed the. Accusations of those horrid *Opinions* that are laid to his Charge,   Which had appeared with much more Evidence , if it had been found that his *Life* had agreed with those *Tenets* : for tho it had not been a just Inference to conclude him guilty of those things , because they were charged on him in the *Bull* , yet one may reckon it almost a sure Inference , that he is not guilty of them , since the *Bull* does not tax him for them.

A

A THIRD LETTER,

Concerning some of the

STATES

OF

ITALY;

And of their present Interest and
Policy.

S I R;

 Threw into my former *Letter*, all those general *Reflections* on the State of *Religion*, and the Maxims of the *Romans*, concerning it, that I could gather together during my Stay at *Rome*. Now I quit that subject, and shall at present en-

entertain you with some *Political Observations*, which will be so much the more acceptable, because I fancy they will be new to you.

But before I go so far as *Italy*, I will give you an account of a very curious *Salt-work*, that I saw in my way to *Italy*, at Sode near *Francfort*. It belongs to Mr. *Malapert*, and has been wrought above 60 *years*; but the present Master of it, as he is a man of great worth, so he is very Ingenious, and has much perfected that, which was managed at a much greater Expence before he undertook it. There rises at the foot of some little *Hills*, which produce a very good *Wine*; a *Spring of Water*, that is so very little brackish to the taste, that one will hardly think it possible to fetch much *Salt* out of it; yet it has such a taste of *Salt*, that there was room for Industry to prepare this *Water*; so that without such an expence in Fire as should eat out the profit, it might turn to a good account; which Mr. *Malapert* seems to have carried as far as is possible. The *Meadow* that lies in the levil with this *Spring*, is Impregnate with *Salt*, *Iron*, *Nitre*, and *Sulphur*: but *Salt* is that which prevails: *first* then, a Pump is put upon this *Spring*, which is managed by a Watermil, and throws up the Water about fifteen Foot high; and then it goes by a Pipe into vast *Machines*, that are made to receive it.

There

There is a great piece of ground Inclofed, in which there are 24 vaft *Chefts* or *Cifterns* for the *Water*, in two *ftories*, 12 in a ftory, the one juft over the other; they are about *feventy* foot long, *twelve* broad, and *two* deep; over every one of thefe, there is a roof of boards, fupported by wooden Pillars, of 12 foot high; which covers them from *Rain*-water, but yet the water within them is in a full expofition to the Sun; thofe roofs are hung with ftraw, upon which fome that manage the work, are often throwing up the *Water*, fo that a great deal of the *phlegme* is Imbibed by the Straw, and the more fixed parts fall down: according to the heat of the Seafon, this Evaporation of the watry parts, goes quicker or flower; there is a *Gage*, by which they *Weigh* the Water, and fo they know how the Evaporation advances; it is of *Silver*, and is fo made, that according to the weight of the *Water*, it finks in it to fuch a depth; & fo by the degrees markt upon it, they know how heavy the *Water* is: according then to the heat of the feafon, and the progrefs of the Evaporation, they let the *Water* out of one *Ciftern* into another, by a *Pipe*, and when it has paft thro the 12 that are in the upper ftory, then it is conveyed down by *Pipes* into the 12 that are below, and in them all they continue ftill to throw up the water upon the Withs of Straw, that are over head.

In a word, this *Evaporation* difcharges the

K   *Water*

Water of so much of its *Phlegm*, that the same quantity of water, that weighed one ounce when it was drawn from the *Spring*, weighs six ounces in this last Chest: and all this rolling about of the Water from Chest to Chest lasts sometimes not above twenty *day's* ; but if the season is only moderately hot, it will be longer a doing ; sometimes it will not be done in a *month's* time : after that the *Water* is brought to a very considerable degree of *Saltness*, it is conveyed into two great *Cauldrons*, that are 13 foot long, ten broad, & $3\frac{1}{2}$ deep ; under which there are vast *Furnaces*, where in a most violent *Fire* of 11 or 12 hours continuance, the *Water* receives its last Evaporation; & when that is done, the *Salt* which is become thick, but is still moist, is taken up in Baskets of Willows, and placed about the wall of the *Furnace* : and so the humidity that remains in it drops out, and it is brought to its last degree of perfection : out of it, a *Tyth* is payed ; of which the *Elector* of *Ments* has one half, and the *City* of *Francfort* the other.   This *Salt* is exceeding good and pleasant to the tast. It is much solider and more like the *Portugal Salt*, than like our *Newcastle salt*. It serveth very well all the uses of the *Kitchin*, and *Table* : but it has not strength enough to preserve things long. There are vast quantities made of it in hot and dry Summers: for the *Chests* are always kept full : and thus all

Fran-

Franconia is furnifhed with *Salt* of its own Production at very moderate rates; for there is fo great a leflening of the Expence of the fire by this conveyance of the water thro fo many Chefts, that it is afforded very cheap. This I thought deferved well that I fhould Interrupt the earneftnefs in which you be, to hear what I have to tell you concerning *Italy*, fo that I hope you will not be ill pleafed with it, efpecially if your curiofity after the Hiftory of nature is as great as it was.

I now go over in one ftep all the *Journey* that I made from hence to *Italy*, which is certainly the *higheft* fcituated Country in *Europe*: for as the *Rhine* and *Danube*, that rife in the *Alpes*, and run down to the *Ocean* and the *Euxine*, fhewes you that all that tract of ground to thofe Seas is a conftant defcent, fo when one comes to the *Alpes*, either on the *French* or on the *German* fide, he is a great many days in climbing up thofe vaft *mountains*, but the defcent on the *Italian* fide is very Inconfiderable. This appears yet more fenfible when one comes from *Turin*, where the afcent up Mount *Senice* is but a work of a few hours: and yet from the height of that *hill*, one is in a conftant defcent till he comes to *Lions*. I will not carry you about *Italy*, to tell you the remarkable things that are there; but will only tell you fome particulars that made the greateft Impreffion on my felf, and

K 2   which

which were not seen by Dr. *Burnet.*

In my way from *Parma* to *Mantua,* I paft at *Guaftale*, which is half way between them, 18 miles diftant from both; where I faw a fcene that furprifed me. This *Town* is fituated on the fouthfide of the *Po*, at half a miles diftance from it: It was a confiderable branch of the Territory of *Mantua,* that was given off to one of the *Cadets* of that *Family*, and was fetled in an intail to the *Heir male.* The beft part of the Revenue of this fmall *Principality*, was a Duty that was payed for all *merchandifes* that went or came upon the *Po*, which when the Trade of *Italy* was in a more flourifhing condition than it is at prefent, was farmed for above Threefcore thoufand *Crowns.* The fituation of this *place* makes it yet much more confiderable than it is in it felf; for as it lies in the neighbourhood of the Principalities of *Parma* and *Modena*, and is not far from the *Popes* Territory, fo it this place is Mafter of the *Po*, by croffing it, the detachments that may be fent out from it are not only in the Territory of *Mantua*, but they may be alfo in a very few hours both in the *Milanefe* and in the *Venetian* Dominion; fo that *Guaftale* in fome refpect may be efteemed the *Center* of all the *States* of *Lombardy.* The Duke of *Mantua* married the Daughter of the laft Duke of *Guaftalé*, who died in the year 1680. and his *Nephew* Don *Vefpafiano Gonzaga*, who was then in

the

the *Spanish* service, was acknowledged to be his undoubted *Heir*: so he came & took peaceable possession of his *Dutchy*: He was extreamly much beloved by his *Subjects*, and thought himself at quiet in the enjoyment of his new Dignity: but all this was soon overturned; for one came to him from the *Court of France*, to let him know, that that *Great King* could not be wanting to his *Ally* the Duke of *Mantua*, to whom *Guastale* belonged of right, his *Dutcheß* being the Daughter and *Heir* of the late *Duke*, and that therefore since he had usurped the just right of another, the *French King* warned him, that if he did not withdraw of his own accord, he would give order to put the D. of *Mantua* in possession. It was to no purpose to argue against all this, and to shew the Messenger that *Guastale* was a *Fee* intailed on the *Heir male*, of which there had never been the least dispute: But reasons taken from the equity of the thing, are seldom thought strong enough to hold the ballance against reasons of State: so the poor *Prince* being in no condition to resist so powerful an Enemy, was forced to abandon his Right, and to withdraw, and he was again entertained by the *Spaniards*. For tho there was a sort of a *fortification* cast about *Guastale* 50 or 60 year ago, yet as that was at best an Inconsiderable defence, so even that was now quite ruined.

K 3

ned. Upon his retiring there came a detache-
ment of 300 Men from *Caſſale*, who took poſ-
feſſion of *Guaſtale*, and continue there to this
day: but this had been no great matter, if it
had not gone further : ſome years paſſed
after the new *Duke* was driven away before
the true deſign of this matter appeared. The
world was firſt to be laid to ſleep. The *Town*
it ſelf is compoſed of about ſix or ſeven thou-
ſand *Inhabitants*; and ſo the ſmall *Garriſon* in
it ſeemed of no great Conſequence, and was
rather an Advantage than a prejudice to the
Town; they were kept in very good order, and
they payed punctually for every thing that
they called for: only they brought the place into the Method of a *Garriſon*; for all muſt come
in and go out of the *Town* only at one Gate.

But in the beginning of the year 1686. the
myſtery of this matter begun to appear : for
Mr. du *Pleſſis* , a French *Engineer* , came
thither, under the pretence of repairing the
old *Fortifications*, and deſigned a Noble and a
Regular *Fortification* : It is to be a *Hexagone*,
with all neceſſary Out-works; and there is a
great *Splanade* that is to be made round the
place, and all the houſes or trees that are within a conſiderable diſtance are to be beat
down. In a word, the deſign is great, and will
be executed in all the exactneſs of the *modern*
Fortification ; ſo that the advantage of the
ſituation, will make it the moſt Important
place

place of *Italy*, and that which will bridle all *Lombardy*, and be able to put it all under Contribution upon every occasion. The Works were begun in April 1686. and ever since they have kept to *men* constantly at work, upon the pay of a *Julio* a day: another year will go near to finish it. And yet tho here the justest ground possible, is given to alarm all *Italy*, none seems to be so much as concerned at it. The *Venetians*, that have at all other times, valued themselves upon their prospect of Danger, even at the greatest distance, either do not see this, or dare not own their fear. It is true, all this is carried on in the name of the D. of *Mantua*: but it is as certain, that tho it lies so near him, he has never been at the pains to go and see it: It has never been so much as once considered by his *Council*; nor is his *Revenue* in such a condition as to bear such an encrease of Expence: and yet it passes among the people there, that this is a great strength, that is to be made to keep the *French* out of *Italy*; and some *Priests* that are corrupted to serve the *French Interests* promote this Fiction. If the *Venetians* look on till this is finished, they will do very well to assure themselves of their new Conquests in the *Morea*, for their Antient ones in the *Terra firma* of *Italy* will probably fail them very quickly.

All those of the *Territory*, who know well that their *Princes* name is only made use of,

for

for the *fortifying* this place , look on with great regret, while they fee a Work advancing fo faft, that is to be a *Citadel* upon all their *Countrey*: of which an Ancient *Perfon* of *Quality*, that is there fpoke to me with fo much feeling, that he could hardly forbear weeping, when he fhewed me that Yoke of Slavery under which they were falling. I faw, during my ftay in *Mantua*, how much all the fenfible people there, are concerned to fee their *Prince* deliver himfelf up fo blindly to the *French Interefts*: they told me, that fince his *childhood* he has been fo befet with the *Inftruments* and *Agents* of that *Court*, that his Inclinations for them are become as another nature in him : he was not out of *Childhood*, when almoft all his *Domefticks*, and his *mafters*, both for *Languages* and *Armes*, were furnifhed him from thence. His putting *Caffale* in the hands of that *Monarch*, was one good Evidence, and now the bufinefs of *Guaftale* is another, to fhew that they have gained fuch an Afcendant over his Spirit, and have Infinuated themfelves fo much into him, in all thofe fatal hours of Liberty which he allows himfelf, that it is not thought he will ftick at any thing that they demand of him, unlefs it be at his own going into *France* ; to which he has been much folicited: but it is not fo much as doubted, that if he goes once into that *Countrey*, he will never come out of it again. So he is

not

not like to be wrought on fo far ; and if it
were not for fome fuch apprehenfion, it is
like enough that he might undertake the
Journey ; for he does not love ftaying in his
Principality fo well, but takes pleafure to
ramble about; and he devefts himfelf often
of the Ceremonies of his *Greatnefs,* that fo he
may take a freer career in thofe *Exerci-
fes*, that he loves better than his *Affairs*:
and a *Prince*, whofe *Revenue* is none of the
greateft,and whofe expence is often Irregular,
who has an active *Envoy* always near him,
and who is ever ready to furnifh him with
Money, falls naturally into a great dependence
on that *Court.*

Of this a very Extraordinary Inftance appeared not long ago, in the Difgrace of the
Marquiffes of *Cannoffe* and *Palliotti* : the firft
of thefe is his *Kinfman*, and has ferved him
now for many years, with as much Fidelity as Affection ; the fecond was *Captain* of
his *Guards*, and *Governour* of the Caftle of
Mantua which commands the *Town*. Thefe
then had the Courage as well as the Fidelity,
to lay before him the Ruin that he was like
to bring upon himfelf as well as upon all *Italy*,
by delivering himfelf up fo intirely to the
French Councils, and by putting them firft
in poffeffion of *Guaftale*, and now fuffering
then to *Fortify* it, which was in effect the
delivering up of his *Principality*, and of all

K 5   his

his *People* to them; who looked upon themfelves as brought already under a *Forreign*
Yoke : they alfo reprefented to him the danger of having almoft no other *Domefticks* but
Frenchmen about him , who were all as fo
many *Spies* upon him , and upon all that were
near him, and that were very exact in giving
the *French Envoy* Mr. *Baumbeau* an account
of every thing that he either faid or did. Thefe
Demonftrances made fome Impreffions on the
Duke , and he promifed to them to find out
an effectuall Remedy to all thofe Evils:
But this was not a fecret very long ; *Money*
and *Spies* find out every thing; and it is poffible
that they who gave the *Duke* thefe faithfull
Advices might have been engaged to it, either
by fome Inftruments of the Court of *Spain*,
or of the Republick of *Venice:* yet the truth
of this is not known, but the *French Envoy*
made a fhift to charge them fo heavily, that
he got them *both* to be made clofe *Prifoners;*
in this condition they were when I was at
Mantua, and no body durft fo much as mention their Names , much lefs Interpofe for
them.

All the *Princes* of *Italy*, are as *Abfolute*
in their own *Dominions* , and as much delivered from all the bonds of *Law* , as fome
greater *Kings* are, fo their *fubjects* are at their
Mercy, both for their *Lives*, *Liberties* , and
Eftates: and this is that from which one may
take

take a sure measure of the weakness of *Italy*. *Subjects* that retain still all the due liberties of humane nature, and that are not under an *Arbitrary* but a *Legall* Government; fight for themselves, as well as for their *Prince*; but if they are already as miserable as they can be, so that a change may perhaps put them in a better condition, but can hardly put them in a worse, they will not much concern themselves in their *Princes* Quarrel, since they only fight for the continuance, if not for the encrease of their Slavery.

But now to return to the Duke of *Mantua*; the *French Envoy* has since that time stuck closer to him than ever; he indeed waits always on him, sometimes acting like an *Officer* of his Houshold, and at other times like the *Governour* of his Person: he made the tour of *Italy* with him this *year*, and waited on him to *Millan*, *Genoa*, *Florence*, *Rome*, *Naples* and *Venice*, where they passed the *Carnavall* together: and he took a most particular care that the *Duke* should meet with none in all those places, that might open his eyes, to let him see the Ruin that he is bringing upon himself; yet after all, one of his *Secretaries*, had still the Integrity and Courage to give him such faithful Councels, as had been fatal to others: yet the *Duke* used him better than he had done the two *Marquisses*: for tho the *French Spies* discovered him likewise, yet, nothing

nothing could be done to hurt him in th
Dukes good opinion, therefore it was refolvec
to take another method to tear fo dangerou
a man from him ; fo he being fent to negotiat
fome bufinefs at the *Court* of *Turin*, was often
invited to go a Hunting, which he refifted for
a great while , tho the *French Ambaffadour*
preffed him much to it ; at laft he was overcome, but his fport was fatal to him; for he
was feifed on , and carried by a fmall *Party*
fent from *Pignarol* as is believed. In fhort,
he is in the hands of the *French*, and it is faid
in *Italy*, that he is clapt up in St. *Margarite* one
of the little *Iflands* in the *Mediterranean fea.*
This matter was at firft highly refented by
the *Duke*, but a little time will fhew whether
the careffes of the *Court* of *France* can foften
him in this matter or not; for if they can lay
him afleep after fuch an Attempt , then all
perfons will conclude that he is fo much in
their power , that none will dare to run
the hazard of undeceiving him any more.

Thofe in the *Mountferrat* feel what a Neighbour *Caffal* is to them; that Imperious way
of proceeding , without having any great regard to Juftice, or to Contracts and Aggree-
ments, that is practifed in *France*, begins to
be felt here likewife: of which many fmaller
Inftances were given me, but I will tell you
two that were more remarkable; when the
Garrifon was firft fetled in *Caffal*, thofe of the
                                        Mount-

Mountferrat held the price of their *Corn* so high, that it was hard to furnish the *Garrison* with Bread : so some of *Piedmont* undertook to supply them for two years at 21 *Livers* the *Ration*, and the bargain being made, they bought in great stores, and so they quickly filled their *Granaries* : upon this some in the *Mountferrat* came and offered to serve the Garrison at 14 *Livers* the *Ration*, upon which the other bargain tho made as sure as any such contract can possibly be made, was broke, and the undertakers were ruined by it.   The other story was, that in order to the building the *Fortifications,* some *Masons* made a bargain at 32 *Livers* such a measure, so they brought together a great number of Workmen, and were at work; when others came and offer'd to perform the work at 28 *Livers*, for which the others had 32 *Livers*, only they demanded a confiderable advance; so the first Bargain was presently broken, to the great loss of the Undertakers : but the 2d Undertakers, that had *Money* advanced them, found they had made a Bargain that was too hard for them to execute, so they ran away with the Money, to the great joy of the Countrey.   He that told me this, said, that perhaps it surprised the *Italians*, who were not yet acquainted with such things; but nothing of that kind would seem extraordinary in *France*, which was so much accustomed to such a way of proceeding

that

that he gave me a particular account of so many, that he had reason to know well, as would fill a Book : but that which touched him most sensibly, was the *Fonds* that was made for an *East-India Company*, to which the *King* gave in *three Millions* , with this positive Assurance, that all the Losses and Dammage of the *Company* should fall on that *Stock*. This was a great encouragment to draw in men, to put *Money* into the stock, and the *Court* set on the Project with so much Zeal, that *Letters* were writ to all the great Bodies and Towns of *France*, that were considered rather as Commands than Desires : yet after all were engaged, upon the first occasion the *Kings* three *Millions* were taken out of the stock, and the rest were left to shift for themselves.

But I must here give you an account of a very Extraordinary Transaction in the *Court* of *Turin* , which is likewise thought an effect of the Authority that the *Councils* of *France* have likewise there. The Marquis *de Pianesse* the *son* of him that set on the *Massacre* of the *Protestants* in the Valleys of *Piedmont* 34 years ago, was in great favour with the late Duke of *Savoy*, but the war of *Genoa* miscarried so in his hands in the year 1672 that the *Duke* could never forgive him that matter; of which the Resentments were so quick when he died, that he left a charge on *Madame Royale*, never to forgive him , nor to Imploy
him

him : he upon his Difgrace retired into *France* and was fo well entertained there, that ne had Intereft enough to procure a Recommendation from the *King* to the Dutchefs of *Savoy* in his favour; but her Excufe was fo reafonable , being founded on the Orders fhe had received from the *Duke* on his Death bed, that there was no reply to be made to it : yet afterwards a *Nephew* of his, the Count *Maffin*, was fo happy in the *Dutcheffes* favour, that he found he only wanted a Head as able as his *Uncles* was to fupport him in that credit, which her favour gave him : and he was fo much in the good graces of *Mad. Royale*, that he at laft prevailed with her to bring his *Uncle* into the chief *Miniftry*; he being certainly one of the ableft men that belongs to that *Court*; and the pretence found to bring this about decently, was, that the *Dutcheffe* did fecretly Intimate to the *Court* of *France*, that fhe found it neceffary to Imploy the Marq. *de Pianeffe*, and therfore fhe defired that the *King* would renew his recommendation of him , which being done, he was received into the *Miniftry*, and had the chief ftroke in all Affairs : he placed another of his *Nephews* about the *Duke*, and fupported him fo that he got very far into his favour, fo Mr. *de Pianeffe* obferving great Diforders in the *Government*, and a great and ufelefs Confumption of the *Revenue*, he Inftructed his *Nephew* that was about the *Duke*

fo well , that he entertained the young *Duke*
often upon thefe heads, who was not then
15 year *old*: he fhewed him how his *Countrey*
was ruined by his *Mothers* ill conduct , and
was always fuggefting to him the Neceffity
of his affuming the *Govornment* , and putting
an end to his *Mothers* Regency, which is a
difcourfe to which all Perfons of that Age
have fuch a natural Inclination , that it was
no wonder if both *Uncle* and *Nephew* came
to believe that the *Duke* hearkned to the Propofition: but the *Duke* thought it too hardy
a thing to venture on it, without confulting
it with fome wifer heads ; upon which Mr.
de Pianeffes Nephew told him , that he would
bring his *Uncle* to him , who would conduct
the matter for him; for tho he had great obligations to *Madam Royale* , yet his Fidelity
to his *Prince*, and his Affection to his *Countrey*
overcame them all. This was a great fur-
prife to the *Duke* , who looked on Mr. *de
Pianeffe* as the perfon in the World, that
was the moft obliged to his *Mother* , and
that was the moft in her *Interefts*: and it was
believed that the prejudice which this gave
him, blafted this whole defign : yet he gave
him feveral Audiences in fecret, and had
concerted with him the whole method, both
of affuming and managing the *Government*:
which was carried on fo fecretly, that there
was no fufpition of the matter , till the day
be-

before it was to break out, and that the *Duke* was to withdraw himself from his *Mother* : but then it was discovered, and the *Duke* to reconcile himself to his *Mother*, sacrificed the *Marq. de Pianeffe* to her resentments: he was not only Disgraced, and put in Prison, but his procefle was made before the Court of *Parliament* of *Chambery*, for having endeavoured to throw the *Government* into a Confusion, by sowing of Division between the *Duke* and his *Mother* : yet he defended himself so well that he was acquitted, but he continues still a Prisoner: upon his Disgrace, there was none that durst oppose himself to *Mad. Royale*, or offer any advices to the *Duke*, so that the *Court* of *Turin* was as absolutely governed by the Directions that were sent from the *Court* of *France*, as if the one had been the *Vaffal*, if not the *Subject* to the other.

I will not prosecute this discourse to tell you that which all *Europe* knows, of the designed Match with the *Infanta* of *Portugal*, by which *Savoy* and *Piedmont* would have undoubtely fallen into the hands of the *French*. The breaking of this, and the *Dukes* being *Poyfoned*, as well as his *Father* had been, tho his youth carried him thro it, are things too well known, for you to be Ignorant of them. It is true, those who *Poyfoned* the present *Duke*, have not been yet Discovered and punished,

L   niſhed,

nished, as those were who poyſoned his *Fa-ther*.   While I was at *Turin* , there was a
diſcourſe, that the *Duke* was reflecting on
the Wiſe Advices that Mr. *de Pianeſſe* had
given him , and that he Intended not only to
bring him out of *priſon* , but to receive him
again into the *Miniſtry* , which is confirmed
to me ſince I left thoſe parts.   There is nothing more Viſible , than that the *Dukes* of
Savoy have ſunk extreamly in this *Age*
from the figure which they made in the *laſt*;
and how much ſoever they may have raiſed
their *Titular* Dignity ;   in having the Title
of *Royal Highneſs* given them , they have loſt
as much in the *Figure* , that they made in the
affairs of *Europe* : and it is now almoſt too
late to think of a Remedy: for *Pignerol* and
Caſſal are two very Inconvenient *neighbours.*
The truth is, the Vanity of this *Title* , and the
expenceful humour that their late *Marria-ges* with *France* has ſpread among them , have
undone them , for inſtead of keeping good
Troops and ſtrong *places* , all the *Revenue*
goes to the keeping up of the Magnificence of the *Court*; which is indeed very
ſplendid.

   I will not ingage in a *Relation* of this laſt
Affair of the *Valleys* of *Piedmont*; for I could
not find particulars enough, to give you that
ſo diſtinctly as you may perhaps deſire it. It
was all over , long before I came to *Turin?*
                                          but

t this I found, that all the *Court* there, were
ıamed of the matter : aud they took pains
on Strangers, not without some affectation,
convince them that the *Duke* was very hard-
drawn to it : that he was long pressed to it, by
: repeated Instances from the *Court* of
ance; that he excused it, representing to
: *Court* of *France* the constant Fidelity of
ıfe people ever since the last *Edict* of *Paci-*
ition, and their great Industry, so that
y were the profitablest Subjects that the
ke had, and that the body of men which
y had given his *Father* in the last War with
ıoa, had done great Service ; for it saved
whole Army : but all these Excuses were
hout effect; for the *Court* of *France* having
ken its own *Faith*, that had been given to
ıeticks, and in that shewed, how true a
ıect it pays to the *Council* of *Constance*, had
ind to engage other *Princes* to follow this
r Pattern of *Fidelity* that it set the world:
ıe *Duke* was not only pressed to extirpate
Hereticks of those *Valeys* ; but this
ıeatning was added, that if he would not
:, the *King* would send his own *Troops* to
rpate *Heresy* ; for he would not only not
r it in his own *Kingdom*, but would even
e it out of his *Neighbourhood*. He who
ıne all this, knowing of what Countrey I
ıadded, that perhaps he would within a
ı while send the like Messages to some o-
ı of his Neighbours. L 2 But

But to return to the expence that is m;
in the *Court* of *Turin*, I cannot forget a (
courfe that I had on this fubject with a *Germ*
that was a man of very good fenfe: he told 1
that nothing ruined the *Empire* fo much,
the great Magnificence which all the *Pri*
affected to keep up in their *Courts*; and
Luxury in which they begun to live, wt
had much corrupted the Antient Simplia
and Gallantry of that great and War
Nation. Not only the *Nobility*, but their v
Princes travel into *France*; and are fo m
taken with the Splendor & Luxury that 1
fee there, that they return home quite fpc
with the ill Impreffions that this make:
them. They carry home with them *Fre.*
Cooks, and all the contrivances of Plea
that are fo much ftudied there, for the v
ting the minds of their *Countreymen*: and
vaft Expence, they not only exhauft 1
Revenue, and ruin their *Subjects*, but
become fo liable to corruption, that if :
Income at home cannot fupport their ch;
both their *Princes* and their *Minifters* ar
duced, as it were to the neceffity of ta
Penfions, from thofe whofe Inftruments
fet on this Luxury, and whofe Penfion:
ftill fupport it, till the *Germans* are
ciently enervated by the Feeblenefs
which all that Luxury muft needs tl
them, and then they will defpife and tra

ıpon them, as much as they do now Court hem. He who told me all this, added, that he little *Princes* of the *Empire*, affected now s much Splendor in their *Courts* as the *Electors* did in the laſt *Age*, and that the *Electors* ived now in as much Magnificence as *:rowned Heads* did formerly. But he carried is Obſervation further, and having ſtaied ɔme conſiderable time both in *Switzerland* nd *Holland*, he added, that Luxury and Exence were wicked things even in *Monarbys*, but they were fatal and deſtructive when ɪey got into *Common-wealths*; of which ɪe Hiſtory of *Lacedemon, Athens,* and above ll of *Rome,* give proofs that are beyond xception; for there is a *Humility,* a *Sobriety,* ɪd a *Frugality,* that is ſo neceſſary for their reſervation; that *Kingdomes* can be better ɪaintained without *Troops* and ſtrong *Places,* ɪan *Common-wealths* without theſe. An Eɪulation in Expence, a Vanity in Clothes, ʹurniture, or Entertainments, are ſo conʹary to all the principles upon which a *Comɪon-wealth* muſt be either built or preſerved, ɪat he ſaid, he thought that the *Dutch* had ɔſt more of their real Strength, by the Proreſs that this Peſt makes among them, than y all the Expence of the *laſt War,* of ʹhich they complain ſo much: and indeed ɪe men of Luxury and Vanity ought to be riven out of *Common-wealths,* as publick

L 3   Ene-

Enemies to the Conſtitution of the *Govern-*
ment : ſince an irregular Profuſion throw
them into Injuſtice and Oppreſſion, and ma
in time expoſe them to the Corruption of.c
ther *Princes*, and diſſolves that Induſtry an
Application for Affairs by which only the
can ſubſiſt: for all the *Maximes* that relate t
a *Common-wealth*, there is none more Ind
ſpenſable, than *that all men regulate their Ex*
pence, *ſo that it may not exceed their Incomt*
and therefore he admired that part of th
Venetian Conſtitution, that regulates th
Expence of their *Nobility*; and concludec
that if the *States* and the *Cantons* did not pr
an effectual ſtop to the Progreſs of thoſe Di
orders among them, the *Figure* that they ha
made in all the Affairs of *Europe*, as it was i
a great degree already Eclipſed among th
Cantons, ſo would ſink apace even in th
States; and this was all that was wantinʒ
to ſet up a *new Monarchy* in the *Weſt*.

But I have got ſuch a trick of making D
greſſions, that I find it is hardly poſſible fc
me to hold long cloſe to a point: there
ſomething in travelling, I fancy, that makes
mans thoughts reel; and that leads his Pen t
wander about as much as his Perſon does: yc
I remember ſtill what drew me into all th
ramble; It was the buſineſs of *Guaſtale*, and th
Court of *Mantua* that led me ſo far about.
will ſay no more to you of the reſt of *Lombar*

dy; nor will I enter into any defcription of *Tufcany*; but fhall only tell you one thing, which both touched me much and pleafed me extreamly.

I need not inlarge to you on the Poverty & Mifery that appears in *Pifa*, where there remains yet enough to fhew what they once were, and how much they are now funk from what they were while they were a *Free State*: but all this is much more fenfible, when one goes from hence to *Lucca*, which tho it has not the advantage of fituation that *Pifa* has, yet is quite another fort of a place. The *Town* is well built, full of *People*, and as full of *Wealth*: the whole foil of this fmall *State* is well Cultivated and is full of *Villages*, all the marks and effects of *Liberty* appear, in an Univerfal Civility, & a generous and frank way of living: This is alfo the place of all *Italy* that is freeſt of all Crimes and Publick Vices; they value themfelves upon nothing but their *Liberty*, of which the *State* is fo Jealous, that the frequent change of their *Magiftrates*, from two Moneths to two Moneths, & the Reftraint in which they are kept while they bear *Office*, they being indeed honorable Prifoners all the while, have preferved that here, which fo many of their Neighbouring *States* have loft: and as *Liberty* is engraven in *Capital Letters*, upon the Publick Buildings of this *State*, fo it appears to be much deeper in all their

L 4   Hearts.

Hearts. One fees the Effects of their *Wealth*, in all their *Publick* works, as well as in the *Fortifications* of this place, which are much better, and better kept than in any place I faw in *Italy*, except *Genoa*. There is on the inward fide of the *Ramparts*, a noble *Plantation*, which is one of the beautifulleft Decorations that belongs to this place; for as there is a confiderable fpace left void between the *Ramparts* and the *Buildings*, fo this is planted all about the whole Town, with feveral rows of Trees, which afford pleafant Walks, and a lovely Shade, which is no fmall matter, where they are expofed to fo hot a Sun.

I come in the laft place to give you an account of *Genoa*, which tho it is not able now to Compete as it did fome Ages ago with the *Republick* of *Venice*, yet is ftill a great Body and full of Wealth; one that comes out of the *Popes Patrimony* and *Tufcany*, into this narrow border that lies between the *Hills* and the *Sea*, fhould expect to find as great a difference between their abounding in People and Wealth, as there is betweeu the foil of thefe two *Countries*: but he finds the change juft contrary to what in reafon he ought to expect: for all this edge of foil, is fo full of *Villages* and *Towns*, and there is fo great a plenty of *Money* and of every thing elfe here, that it Amafes a *Traveller* no lefs, than the abandoned ftate of thofe other places.   The

The numbers of the subjects of this *Republick*, are estimated to 330000 *Persons*; which are thus reckoned up; In the Town of *Genoa* it self there are about 80000. *Persons* : in the *Villages* and *Towns* that lie *Westward* there are 120000. and 30000. in those that lie to the *East* : and the *Inhabitants* of the Island of *Corsica* are reckoned to be 100000. They keep two small *Forts* in *Corsica* , one at *Calvi* on that end that looks to *Genoa* , and another at *Boniface* on the other end that looks to *Sardinia*; for they have let S. *Fiorenza* and some other small places go to ruin. These two are considerable in themselves, and command two very good Harbours; yet as the building in *Calvi* are too much exposed and too high, so *Boniface* is under a high Ground, that is within musket shut of it, and that commands it: these places are now in a sad condition, ill kept, and ill furnished both with Men and Ammunition, so that they could not make a great Resistance , there being but 150 men in *Calvi*, and 200 in *Boniface*; and it is believed , that the reason of their letting S. *Fiorenza* go to ruin, is, the Greatness of the Place, and the Expence of keeping it. The *Corses* are extreamly brave , and have a Rage in their courage, that would be much more valueable and usefull than it is if they were more governable, and could be brought under an exact Discipline : but they are unruly ,

L. 5   and

and as apt to Mutiny, when they fee no Enemy, as to fight well when it comes to that.
The compafs of the *Fortification* of *Genoa* is
an amafing thing; for it runs all along the hills
in a compafs of many miles, I was told it was
above 15 mile, & in the Expence that has been
laid out on this and on the two *Moles*, chiefly
the new one, one fees that this *State* fpares
nothing which Publick fafety or the Conve-
nience of Trade do require : thefe Publick
Works has run the *Republick* into a vaft debt;
for they owe above Nine Millions of *Crowns*
that are upon the *Bank*, befides feveral other
debts, in particular their great Debt to St.
Georges Houfe ; the greateft part of the *Revenue* of this *State* ftands engaged for the *Intereft* that they pay, fo that tho the whole
Revenue amounts to 1200000 *Crowns*, they
reckon that 900000 *Crowns* of this is engaged,
fo that they have only three hundred thoufand *Crowns* clear for their whole Expence,
which is fo fmall a matter, that it is no wonder if they are in a low condition, and can do
little upon fo narrow a fond: their *Revenue* rifes
chiefly out of an *Excife* that falls fo equally
upon all the *Subjects* of this *State*, that they
reckon that every man in *Genoa*, payes fix
Crowns a year to the *State*. The whole Land
Forces of this *State* were but 3500 men, yet
of late they have raifed them up to 4000 men;
of which 2500 are the Garrifon of the *City*,
                                                    and

and there are 600 in *Savona*, which after the City it felf is the moft Important place that belongs to this *State* : the extent of the whole Countrey, that goes by the name of the *River of Genoa*, is 180 *miles*, of which 120 lie *Weftward*, and 60 lie *Eaftward*; the *Mountains* that are almoft Impaffible are thought a fufficient Defence to cover them from their Neighbours in *Lombardy*, and from the Duke of *Savoy*, and the State of *Millan*. It is true, they have one *Fort* called *Gavi*, that is 25 miles diftant from the *Town*, which has all the advantages of fituition that are poffible for keeping the Paffes thro the Mountains: but as they keep only a Garrifon of 120 men in it, fo all things in it are fo neglected, that it could make no confiderable Refiftance to an Enemy that could attack in vigoroufly. In fhort, the ftrength of this *State* is very Inconfiderable, their *Souldiers* are ill Difciplined, their *Officers* want Experience, and they have no good *Engineers* ; the New *Mole* is indeed a vaft work, built out into the *Sea* feven fathom deep, and there are an hundred pieces of *Cannon* on it to defend the Old Mole; their Naval forces confift in fix *Galleys*, and and two Men of *War*; but thefe are not kept as Ships of War, but are Imployed rather as Merchant-men, fo that they not only bear their own Expence, but bring in an Overplus to the *State*.

Finale,

Finale, which is the only Seaport that belongs to the State of *Millan,* is a poor abandoned *Village* without either Fortification or Garrison, nor do the *Spanish Galleys* come there any more ; but make *Genoa* it self their Step, and Passage between *Spain* and *Millan* : so that an attempt upon *Genoa* was indeed the taking of all the *Milanese,* since the communication between *Spain* and it, being now thro *Genoa,* whensoever this Republick falls into the hands of the *French,* all the *Millanese* must fall of it self, or rather indeed all *Italy,* must needs fall with it.

This is as far as I could understand it the outward force of *Genoa* : for it can expect little from its *Allies,* it having none at all beside *Spain* : and the Slowness and Feebleness of that *Court,* are too visible to give any *State* great Courage that has no other support besides this to depend on : As for their Neighbours in *Italy,* they have no sort of Commerce with them ; for they pretend to a degree of Precedence, equal to the *Venetians* : and to have the respect of a *Crowned Head* pay'd to them, and this cuts off all Communication with the other *Courts* of *Italy,* who consider *Venice* in another manner than they do *Genoa.* As for *Spain,* they have all possible Engagements with it : many of the richest Families of *Genoa* have great *Estates* in the *Milanese,* and the other Dominions of the *King* of
Spain ;

Spain; fo that they muft upon their own account be true to the Interefts of that Crown, and *Spain* is as much concerned in their prefervation as in any of its own Provinces, fince it defends their Empire in *Italy*; fo that *Genoa* and *Spain* are now infeparably united to one another, by their mutual Interefts.

But I come next to give you fome account of the Inward ftate of *Genoa*. It is known, that the Liberty was reftored to them, by the moft earneft Interceffion of that great *Captain*, and gallant Countrey-man, *Andreas Doria*, whofe Statue, in remembrance of this, is fet up in an open place in their *Town* : this was in the year 1528. yet tho from that time they had their Government in their own hands, they were ftill obliged to let a Squadron of the *Spanifh Gallys*, ftand in their *Arfenal*, who kept then a Fleet of about 80. *Gallys*, fo that till *Spain* was fo much funk from its former Greatnefs, that it was no more a Terrour to any of its *Neighbours*, *Genoa* was ftill in great dread of having their Liberty fwallowed up by them, and therefore they do not reckon their entire Liberty but from the year 1624. or 1625. that they faw themfelves out of all Danger from any of their Neighbours : *France* was not then begun to grow ftrong at Sea, and *Spain* was ftrong no where; fo that fince that time, till

France

France began to put out great Fleets, and that they had such a dreadful Neighbour of *Touloun*, they were safe and at quiet: but they fell under the common Disease of all *Commonwealths,* when they are long in Peace, and while their Commerce flourishes ; a Spirit of Insolence and of Faction began to spread it self over the whole *Town*, which was grown to such a height, that in the *Project* that was offered to the *Court* of *France*, shewing the easiness of this Conquest (of which I have seen the Copy) the Divisions and Factions amongst them are proposed, as the chief ground upon which they founded the Probability of the ruin of that *Common-wealth.*

There are *three* sorts of Persons in *Genoa*, the *Nobility*, the *Citizens*, and the *Inferior People.* There are two Ranks of *Nobility*, the one is of the more *Antient Families*, the other is of those who have been chosen and raised up to that Dignity of late. It is true, the Aggreement that was made in the year 1576. between them, is exactly observed, by which the Government and the Publick Imployments are to be equally divided between them : but yet there is so great a height of Pride kept up among the Ancient Families, that they will not Inter-marry with the other, and think it a diminution to them, to enter into any Familiarity with them ; and even to keep them Company : this on the other hand kindles

kindles an Indignation in thofe latter *Families*, when they fee themfelves fo much defpifed by the other. The Ancient *Families* have a neceffary Dependence upon the *Crown* of *Spain*, by the great Eftates that they have in their Dominions; but the others, whofe Eftates lie rather in Money, which either is in the Bank, or that runs out in Exchange or Trade, they are concerned in nothing but in the prefervation of their *Bank*, and by confequence in their Liberty; for none can doubt but that if they fell in the power of another *Prince*, the Debts on the *Bank* would be but ill payd. Thus the *Nobility* ftand divided into two Factions, which difcover their Animofities to one another upon very many occafions: for *Publick Imployments* are fought after here, with as much Intrigue as elfewhere. I will give you only one Inftance of this, becaufe it is both very refined, and it related to that *Doge*, whofe Government was fo unhappy both by the *Bombarding* of *Genoa*, and by his own going to *Verfailles* to ask Pardon. He himfelf was a Man of a quiet temper, that did not afpire; but his *Wife* could not be fatisfied till he was *Doge*, and fhe *Dogeffe*: fo fhe fet fo many Machines at work, that after the feveral tours, that the matter made in the many *Ballottings*, it came to the fixing of the laft *three* out of whom the *Doge* was to be chofen: and her Husband

was

was one of them ; but there being one of the three, of whom she was very apprehen-five, she engaged one of her Friends, to seem so assured of his *Election*, as to lay considerable wagers with several of the *Electors*, who were likeliest to favour him, that he should be chosen : now they having a greater mind to win their Betts, than to promote their Friend, gave their *Votes* in favour of him, that was upon that made *Doge*.

The 2ᵈ body in *Genoa* is that of the *Citizens*, who seem to be extreamly weary of the Insolence of the *Nobility* ; and there are many among them, that think themselves no way Inferiour to them, neither in the Antiquity, nor in the Dignity of their *Families*. They do also complain of a great Injustice done them by the *Nobility* ; for in the agreement made between the *Nobility* and the *Citizens*, in the year 1528. one *Article* was, that every year *ten Citizens* should be according to their merit received into their body. It is certain, that if this had been observed, the *Nobility* of *Genoa* had become by this time so common, that this would have sunk its dignity extreamly : but instead of doing this *yearly*, it is now done but once in 30 *years* : so the *Citizens* complane much, that this Encouragment and Recompence of *Merit* is now withdrawn. The *Nobility* pretend on the other hand, that by that Agreement, they are
only

nly enabled to make an *Annuall* promotion,
ut that they are not obliged to it : and I was
old, that the Originall *Record* of that Agree-
nent, could not be found now; and no doubt
t has been deſtroyed by the Order of the *Se-
nate*. In ſhort, the *Citizens* have ſo great an
verſion to the *Government*, that it was generally thought that they would eaſily be
nrevailed on to ſhake it off, and to throw
hemſelves rather into the Armes of another
Prince, who would certainly have very ſoon
rampled upon them all equally; for it is too
ommon a thing, to ſee in all thoſe Inteſtine
Factions, that angry and ill-natured men,
onſider the laſt Injury, more than all other
hings: and are ready to ſacrifice all to their
Reſentments: and are ſo intent upon their
Revenges, that often they will not look
nto the Conſequences of what they do,
ut go on, which way ſoever the Anger of
he *Faction* drives them : and thoſe who are
viſe enough, to make their own Advantage
f thoſe Quarrels, and that are dextrous
nough to manage them artificially, make
ommonly thoſe *parties* take their turns in
ſing one another ill, in which they know
now to find their account : and as this ob-
ervation holds often in *Colder Climates*, ſo
n a *Countrey* where revenges are very much
tudied and gratified, no wonder if this was
nuch relied on. The third rank is of the
Tradeſ men and Rabble, who have their chief,

M   depen-

dependance upon the great *Nobility* : but they are a Vicious and diffolute fort of *People*, as any are in the world.   And indeed all *Genoa* is fo extreamly corrupt, fo Ignorant, and fo brutal, and fo little acquainted with the true Notions of *Government*, that here is a *Common-wealth* degenerated to fuch a degree, that it cannot refift a confiderable fhock.   The *Subjects* are exceffively Rich, tho the *State* is Poor : and this appears both in the Magnificence of their *Buildings*, which is beyond Imagination, and in the great *Wealth* that is in their *Churches* and *Convents*, which feemed to me to be beyond what is in *Venice* it felf.

A fenfible man that I knew there told me, that as there was among them a fort of Impunity to all Kind of Vice, fo their grofs Ignorance made them Incapable to conduct their *State*; for while their *Wealth* blew them up, with that Pride that it commonly produces in mean Souls, and when their Intrigues brought them into a confiderable fhare of the *Government*, they fatisfied themfelves with carrying on the Interefts of their own *Cabal*, and depreffing thofe that oppofed them, without opening their minds to fo great a thought, as that of correcting or fecuring their *Common wealth*.   They neither had Heads nor Hearts capable of a vigorous Defence : and they knew nothing of what was doing abroad; but contented themfelves

with

with minding the Interest of their *City Fa-*
ctions. He added, that when a *Common-*
wealth fell once into this Disease, it was in
a much worse state, than any to which
the Rigour even of an unhappy War, could
reduce it : as a man whose Vitals are Inwardly corrupted, is in a much worse condition, than he that has received many Wounds;
Nature may bring him thro the one, tho
he had lost ever so much blood; whereas it
must sink under the other: so all the mischief
that could befall a *Common-wealth* could
hardly destroy it, if it retain'd the Inward
vigour of its first *Maximes* and *Constitution:*
and he did not stick to say, that as high as
the *States of Holland* were now in holding
the *ballance of Europe,* if their *Towns* fell once
into established *factions,* if *Learning* sunk
among them, so that their *Magistrates* grew
Ignorant, chiefly of the *Affairs* of *Europe,*
if they came to have a *Magistracy,* that had
not the right understanding of *War,* and the
Courage with which some practice in *Mili-*
tary matters Inspire men, and if their *Wealth*
swelled them up to an Unreasonable Pride,
and that men rise more upon the little Intrigues of *City Factions,* than upon true merit;
whensoever, he said, the *States* fell into this
disease, then the strength of that *Republick*
was gone; and tho they might subsist after
that longer or shorter, according to the Conjuncture of Affairs, yet one might reckon

them

them to be in their decline, which muſt end
in a moſt certain Ruin to them, either within
doors, or from abroad.

I have now told you enough to let you
ſee how reaſonable a Project it was to ſend a
fleet againſt ſo feeble a *body*; which without
moſt prodigious Errors in the management,
could not have miſcarried: and this is ſo clear,
and ſo confeſſed by every man in *Genoa*, that
one rather Wonders how they found a way to
conduct it ſo ill. The *man* that formed the
whole project was *Stiven Valdyron* ot *Niſmes*,
and a *Proteſtant*, who is a perſon of a very good
Underſtanding, and having lived above 12
years in *Genoa*, had time enough not only to
raiſe a very good Eſtate out of his Trade,
but to ſee into the whole Feeblenefs of that
Government. I converſed long and much with
him: and having ſince that time been in *Genoa* it ſelf, I have ſeen ſo clearly the truth of
all that he told me, that I may now aſſure
you of all that I learnt from him. He had
a ſtrange affection to his *Great Monarch*,
and fancied that the obligations of raiſing
his Glory, was ſuperiour to all other: and no
doubt he reckoned to find his own account
in it, if he could have been the occaſion of
making the *King of France* Maſter of *Genoa*:
therefore he drew up the whole *Project*, and
ſhewed both of what Importance the thing
was, and how eaſily it might be executed:
for I have a *Copy* of the whole *Scheme*, which
                                             Mr.

Mr. *St. Olon* sent to the *Court of France*, of which Mr. *Valdyron* was indeed the *Author*; the design being entertained , *St. Olon* had an Intimation given him, to withdraw some day's before the *French fleet* came before the *Town*. But *Valdyron* was left to try his hard fate; for as soon as the *Fleet* began to do Acts of Hostility, *Valdyron*, who had been known to be much with *St. Olon*, was clapt in *Prison*, and while he was in it , a *Bomb* broke thro his Prison, but did him no hurt, only the violent noise it made weakned the Tympan of his *Ear* so much , that he lost his hearing of one side.

But he, as well as all *Genoa*, fancied they were lost, and that the *French* must be certainly Masters of the *Place* in a few hours. The Consternation and Confusion was so great, that if at first a great shower of *Bombs* had been thrown into the *Town*, and a descent had been made, they had certainly succeeded; for the *people* were in such a disorder, that the *Magistrates* were not regarded; and indeed many of them shewed as much fear as the rabble did. But the *French*, instead of beginning vigorously at first , threw in one Bomb , and after some hours *another*; and so went on slowly for a day or two; in which time, the *People* began to get into order , and to take heart : and now their first fear, turned to a Rage against the *French*; so that when they made a descent, they found

such

such a Refiſtance, that they were forced to go back to their *Ships*, having left behind them 500 of their beſt *Men* : and the *Fleet* continued *Bombarding* the *Town*, till they had ſhot all their *Bombs*; and when their ſtore was ſpent, they fail'd away, having laid a great many noble *buildings* in ruines.

The *morality* of this way of proceeding, was ſomewhat hard to be found out : the *Italians* do not ſtick to ſay, it was an *Aſ-ſaſſinat*, when without Warning or procee-ding in the way of a fair *War*, a *fleet* came and ſurpriſed and burnt a *Town* : but the Conduct was as extraordinary, as the Action it ſelf was honorable and worthy of a MOST CHRISTIAN KING.

It was pleaſant to hear a *Spaniard*, that belonged to the Count of *Melgar* talk of this matter : he ſaid, that in this, *France* had acted as it had done on many other occaſions, in which tho it had the favourableſt conjuncture poſſible, it had done nothing ſuteable to what might have been expected; for tho they had here a calm *Sea*, for four dayes, which is a very Extraordinary thing in the *Bay* of *Genoa*, that is almoſt alwayes in a *Storm*, and tho they had ſurpriſed the *Town*, that had not the leaſt apprehenſion of ſuch a Deſign, and found them in a condition not likely to have reſiſted a much ſmaller Force; yet he ſaid, that Feeble neſs which had appeared upon many othe occaſions, ſhewed it ſelf likewiſe here ; ſince

this

this great Expedition failed, and the Reproach of firſt attempting it , and then Miſcarrying in it, was ſtudied to be carried off by this , that the deſign was only to *Chaſtiſe Genoa*, at which there is not a *man* in the *Town* that does not laugh. He upon this took a great compaſs for theſe laſt twenty *years* backwards, to ſhew that there was nothing extraordinary in all this *Reign*, that had been the Subjeſt of ſo many *Panegyricks*, unleſs this may be reckoned extraordinary, that there has been ſo little progreſs made, when they had the faireſt opportunities poſſible: an Infant *King* of *Spain*, and a feeble *Council*, and a Diſtraſtion in the *States* of *Holland*; ſo that the firſt Succeſſes that were the Effeſts of the weakneſs and ſurpriſe of thoſe that were attackt, are rather a Reproach than a Glory to a *Reign*, that has underſtood ſo ill how to ſerve it ſelf of thoſe advantages, that had nothing of the Greatneſs of a *Conquering* Genius in it ; and where the *Miniſtry* ſhewed rather an exaſtneſs in executing little Projeſts, than a largeneſs of Soul in laying vaſt ones. I could not but be pleaſed to ſee a *Spaniard*, find ſomewhat that entertained his Pride in the Contempt of the *French*, at the ſame time that the low eſtate of their Affairs, made him feel the depreſſion of their own *Empire* as much as the progreſs of the Great Monarch of *France*.

But now I cannot but tell you the reſt of

M 4   *Valdy-*

Valdyron's Story: as foon as the F
gone, the Government of *Genoa*
examin him, but he ftood to his d
faid, he knew nothing: all his E
feifed on and diffipated, and he h
four or five times put to the ftrapa
was done by tying his hands behin
and fetching them over his Head,
joynted his Armes and Shoulder-b
moft terrible manner, yet he had
nefs to ftand it out: and fo they c
nothing from him: but as foon as
of *France* underftood, that both he
ral other *Frenchmen*, that lived
were put in Prifon, the *Refident*
was clapt up at *Paris:* and when
tures were made to accommodate t
Valdyron was no more ill ufed,
fome Months he was fet at Lib
his *Eftate* was quite loft: yet h
France, not doubting but that fo
vice, and fuch fevere Suffering, w
procured him fome confiderable
but after he had languifhed ther
year, he got a *Penfion*, that was j
to keep him alive, of two hundre
and even that was ftopt, 'as foon it
that he was of the *Religion*, till he
This piece of Gratitude for fuch
that had coft him fo dear, was no
nary Encouragement for others to
he had done. Yet I who knew him

almost two years; could not but admire the wonderful Zeal he had for the Glory of his *King* ; for in the midst of all his Misery, and of all the Neglect he met with, having fallen from so flourishing a condition , he could never be brought to think that he had done foolishly : but was rather proud of it, that he had formed so sure a Scheme , for putting *Genoa* into his *Masters* hands: & this he said often to me, when he was so poor, that he did not know where to dine. The affinity of the matter , makes me call to mind a conversation that I had at *Rome* , with two of the Old *Magistrates* of *Messina*; who had been men that bore a great stroak in that *Town* , during the *Revolt* : and were then reduced to the misery of accepting a Charity. They told us, that all the *Oaths*, that Mr. *de Vivonne*, and Mr. *la Fueillade* , swore to them in the *Kings* name, as well as in their own, never to abandon them, which were made upon the *Sacrament*, besides whole Valleys of *Oaths*, that Mr. *la Fueillade* made them from morning to night, while he was among them , it seems went for nothing, but matters of form : yet they said, they thought the *French Ministry* would have considered the *Kings Interests*, if they had no regard to his *Honour*. They added, that if the *King* of *France*, when he found the War of *Messina* lay heavy upon him, had sent to *Spain*, and offered to that *Court*, as a pledge of the Peace that he was offering them at *Nimmegen*,

to

to put *Messina* again in to their hands, provided they would grant an *Indemnity* for what was past, and a Confirmation of their Antient *Priviledges*, of which he himself would be the *Garand*, this they said the *Spaniards* would have without doubt, accepted as something come to them from Heaven : and if the matter had ended thus, as it would have been highly honourable for the *King*, so it would have given him the dependance both of *Sicily* and *Naples*, and have kept them still in a disposition to throw themselves into his hands : whereas in the way that their business ended, if there should be in any time hereafter, a provocation given in those parts to *revolt*, they would sooner throw themselves into the Armes of the *Turk*, if he should be again in a condition to protect them, than of those who had abandoned them in so strange a manner, taking no care neither of the *Priviledges* of the *Town* in general, nor of those particular *Persons*, who had rendred themselves unpardonable to the *Spaniards*. It is true, some were brought away to *France*, the *two* that I have mentioned were of that number, and had small *Pensions* assigned them, which were but ill payed: and because some of them had not patience enough to bear such an unlooked for *Usage*, but complained freely of it, a pretence was taken from thence, to *banish* them all out of *France*; so that ever since they have suffered a great deal of Misery. I will not

digress

digrefs fo far as to give you an account of
that whole *Revolt*, which they juftified to us,
from the great *Priviledges* of their *Town*,
which were indeed fuch as made it a fort of
a *Common-wealth*: that had a right to defend
it felf againft thofe manifeft Infractions with
which they charged the *Spaniards*. They
told us, that the Confifcations of *Meffina* had
amounted to twenty *Millions*: and yet for all
that the *King of Spain* was not much the richer by their Ruin ; for the *Vice-Roy* and
Government of *Sicily*, pretended to exhauft all
by a *Citadel* that they are building : and by
fome other publick Works. In Conclufion,
the two poor *Meffineffes*, feeing a *Dutchman*
in our Company, turned the Difcourfe to
him, and wifhed him to warn his *Countreymen*, by their Fate, how much fome *Courts*
ought to be relied on.

And now I have done with all the *Political
Obfervations*, that I could make in *Italy*. But
as I begun this *Letter* with one piece of *Natural Hiftory*, I will end it with another. The
firft was a way of preparing of *Salt*, and the
fecond is a new way of preparing of *Vitriol*,
which was lately fet up in the *Sulfatara*,
near *Puzzolo*. It has not been long enough
a going, to enable one to judge how it will
fucceed ; but yet all things are very promi-
fing; and that which gives a good Profpect
of it, is, that all is done without the expence
of any *fire*. The Method of it is this. There
                                                    are

are several *Cisterns* made in that great Bottom of the *Sulfatara*, of great *stones* Cemented very close: into these all the *Rain* both of that Bottom, and of the little Hills that are round it does fall , which is impregnated with *Vitriol* : they do also lay a great many Tiles and Bricks before all those Vents, that the Fire which is in this Soil makes: and where the Smoke comes out, with so rapid a violence; so that this Smoke passing thro these Bricks, leaves a great deal of *Sulphur* and *Vitriol* upon them : and these Bricks are washed in those *Cisterns*, and by this means the *Water* becomes impregnated with *Vitriol*: then they put the Water into *Coppers*, which they set over those violent hot Eruptions; so that this serves as a Fire, to evaporate the Phlegm, and so they find quantities of *Vitriol*. The revenue of this goes to the *Annunciata* of *Naples* : and they begin to promise themselves great advantages from it : but a little time will shew this, as well as greater matters. I will add no new trouble, to that which the length of this *Letter* must needs have given you: so I will conclude, without any other Formality , but that of assuring you that I am,

.S I R,

Your most humble Servant.

POST-

POSTSCRIPT.

SInce I added a *Postscript* to my *two* former *Letters*, I intend to make this so far of a piece with them, as to conclude this likewise with one ; for I find, looking over the little Notes that I took, a Particular that had escaped me, and yet it seems to deserve to be mentioned: and since I have not brought it into my *Letters*, I have resolved to make a *Postscript* express for it.

There is a little *Town* in the *Appennins*, about 25 miles from *Rome* , called *Norcia*, near which there is a considerable *Abbey* , which belongs now to a *Cardinal*. This *Town*, tho it lies within the *Popes* Territory, yet has such great Priviledges still reserved to it , that it my pass in some sort for a free *Common-wealth*. They make their *Lawes*, and choose their own *Magistrates*; but that which is the most extraordinary part of their Constitution , and that is the most exactly observed, is, that they are so jealous of all *Priests*, and of their having any share in their *Government* , that no man that can either read or write is capable of bearing a share in their Government : so that their *Magistracy*, which consists of 4 *Persons*, is alway's in the hands of *Unlettered* Men, who are called there *Li quatri Illiterati* : for they think the least

ten-

ERRATA.

Page 6. line 16. dele *of.* P. 9. l. 22. po̧rtion r. *pro-proportion.* P. 16. l. 18. after and r. *upon.* P. 22. l. 4. dele *that.* P. 27. l. 7. r. *that was.* P. 34. l. 23. cited r. *said.* P. 36. l. 19. is r. *it.* P. 38. l. 18. dele *a.* P. 47. l. laſt. r. *ſlippers.* P. 48. l. 9. fling. r. *fling.* l. 20. hear r. *bear.* P. 70. l. 26. is r. *were.* P. 82. l. 11. ſtrong r. *ſtrange.* P. 83. l. 8. or r. *of.* P. 85. l. 9. Sr. r. *St.* P. 87. l. 16. 235. r. 35. P. 89. l. 3. r. *Damnatos.* P. 130. l. 11. meer. r. *we.* P. 137. l. 10. where r. *when.* P. 169. l. 18. shut r. *Shot.* P. 171. l. 18. in r. *it.*

www.ingramcontent.com/pod-product-compliance
Lightning Source LLC
Chambersburg PA
CBHW020623030726
47497CB00007B/2393